The

# Lightbringer

Douglas Scaddan

ISBN: 978-0-9683071-4-4

The

# Lightbringer

Douglas Scaddan

This is a work of fiction. Names, characters, places, and incidents either are the product of the author's imagination or are used fictitiously, and any resemblance to actual persons, living or dead, events, or locales is entirely coincidental.

Published by Douglas Scaddan Publishing
Cover Art by Douglas Scaddan

ISBN: 978-0-9683071-4-4

# *DEDICATION*

There are far too many people to thank or acknowledge for this work. It's the ulmination of many years and many people. Each character in this book can be traced back to a living person that I call a friend. As I wrote this, I smiled and remembered them fondly.

My Mother was instrumental in bringing this to fruition. The first, very rough copy was first published by Essence Publishing back in the mid '90s. I was never completely satisfied with it and have wanted to rework it for years. I would play with it for a while and then put it away and then play some more a year or so later. My Mother gave an attention to detail with art and my appreciation for all art forms. Thank you.

Sarah. You know why.

To God be the glory.

# Praise for The Janitor

This book may be a work of fiction, but the voice of Scaddan's narrative makes it feel as real as my own life. I was challenged by this book, reintroduced to the love of God and simple faith, and filled with tears as I related to the pains and joys of my new friends off these pages. I recommend this book to anyone who can spare a few minutes for a short read.

- Josh (Amazon.ca user)

# Praise for The Trustee's Manual

The author's knowledge and application of scriptures makes The Trustee's Manuel indispensable for basic trustee training. His experience and research enables an informed presentation delivered in an engaging style. Purposefully, he removes lingering doubts about the spiritual role of Christians entrusted with civic stewardship on behalf of congregations. Believers will be able to grasp the essential role of trustee without feeling the need to be a bible scholar. I highly recommend this gem.

# Also by Douglas Scaddan

The Trustee's Handbook

The Janitor

# Prologue

The church stood alone in the dark. Its high peak reached for the sky, like a child reaching for the hand of a father. The snow fell in torrents all around and, giving off what little light there was, streetlights stood in mute testimony to the passage of an evil night. The man looked out along the street; his long, black hair blew in the wind against the stark white snow. A long, black trench coat hugged his body and flapped like broken crow's wings around his legs. Beside the church was the University of Windsor, a higher place of learning, with it's tall spires reaching up and the hallowed halls and auditoriums dedicated to knowledge. The man smiled. Fools, he thought, if only they knew what real learning was. The secrets of the universe were his to command and the planes of self-awareness were his playgrounds. That was the meaning of true knowledge. Knowledge was power, and this man was very powerful.

He opened the door to the church and walked in, and the scent of ancient wood and newly burnt incense gripped his nostrils. He felt a momentary pang of panic as he thought the priest who stood at the front of the sanctuary might know the reason he was here; then he pulled his leather gloves tighter onto his hands and his resolve hardened. He walked up the centre aisle of the church. The high domed roof of the glorious church echoed his footsteps, as if the very floorboards were knocking to warn all within earshot of his unholy presence. The priest turned angrily to face the intruder, and dropped the bowl he was holding as he moved to face the man. Blood, splattered on the floor and rolled in small puddles over the black circle on the floor, the bowl rolled around on it's edge, finally coming to a stop and flopping to the ground. The stranger eyed the blood and the bowl with a strange smile that never touched his eyes.

"Who are you?" the priest demanded, pulling his shoulders up and gaining some strength, and pride, in his voice.

The man laughed and strode slowly up the aisle. He waved his hands in the air as if leading an orchestra, until he was standing only a few feet from the priest and the small pool of blood. "You don't remember me, old man?" he said in a sing-song voice. "We were enemies once, a long time ago. Now, I see that we are alike, you and I."

"There is nothing similar about us!" the priest yelled, his voice catching and breaking the louder he got. Then he glanced down at the splattered blood on the floor. "I am merely trying to become more knowledgeable so that I might serve the Lord better," he said weakly.

"You lie, Priest!" the man yelled, spittle flying into the old man's face. “You have found the secret to real power! You have tasted the forbidden fruit of knowledge and desire more. You desire as I do, priest. You and I are joined forever in the bonds of forbidden knowledge.”

“I am no servant of Satan,” the priest said weakly.

"LIES!" The man screamed. “You are a servant of the great lord Satan! But because you deny him, because you don’t worship but steal his knowledge and power,” he stepped in closer to the priest and hissed softly in his face. “You. Will. Burn. In. Hell.” The man pulled a hammer out of his coat and swung at the priest, who slipped in the blood and fell to his back, holding his blood smeared hands up to protect his body.

"Please, don't," the priest said as he tried to shuffle back. "Please have mercy!"

"Mercy?" the man said thoughtfully. "Doesn't your God speak of mercy?"

The priest screamed as the dark haired man drove the hammer into his chest. Blood spurted from around the hammer head and splashed on the floor and the dark man’s clothes. He covered the priest's mouth with his gloved hand until the priest stopped jerking, his eyes rolled back in his head and blood slipped between his fingers. There was a part of him that wanted to remove the gloves and feel the blood between his fingers.

Then he began his evil work. The floor soon became red as the sound of a hammer hitting nails rang out into the flickering semi-darkness of the church. Then, as calmly as if he had merely talked to the priest about the violent weather outside, he quietly left the church, hugging his blood stained clothes to his body. The blood froze almost instantly and cracked a few small pieces falling to the snow. He was worried for a second, then realized that the blood chips were almost immediately covered by snow.

He walked, strolled really, to the old house on Donnelly Street, whose tilting porch and dirty windows seemed to be a crooked smile to the murderer's eyes. Ripping open the front door he stepped in and stood with his bloody clothes hanging from his body. As the frozen blood thawed, the red liquid fell to the hardwood floor and splattered in a spider-web. A thin man dressed in black stood from a chair where he was reading a book.

"Is it done, Robert?" the man asked, setting his book on a table. His voice betrayed a slight tremor of fear.

Robert stripped off the bloody coat and dropped it on the floor.

"The first is dead," he said simply. with a wicked smile. He stepped out of his pants and stripped off the rest of his clothes, dropping them in the pile with the coat. "I'll be in the shower if anyone needs me." Robert walked, naked, past the man and into a small bathroom by the kitchen at the back of the house. His flesh was white, almost painfully so. The taut muscles corded and told of many hours in a gym.

The man in black stepped over to the bloody coat and stood over it, thinking for a moment, his eyes locked onto the blood. Then, he suddenly nodded, as if making a momentous decision. Rummaging into the kitchen he grabbed a wooden spoon and put the coat and the other bloody clothes into a garbage bag. Then the man in black went down to the basement and unlocked a safe concealed in a dark corner of a small library.

"Your lust for blood may be your undoing, Robert," the man muttered as he placed the bag in the safe. "But I shall not let you take me with you."

As he returned upstairs, Robert stepped out of the bathroom, clean, and no longer stinking of blood, a dark blue towel was wrapped around his waist, which flared up to wide shoulders draped with black hair. He turned to the man in black as he dried his hair. Noticing that the bloody pile of clothes was gone, asked, "Raven, what have you done with my clothes?"

"It would have been unwise to have kept them," Raven said, nonchalantly looking up from his book. "I burnt them in the fireplace in the basement."

Robert studied Raven's face for a moment, as if measuring his worth, then he suddenly nodded his approval. "Good, the less existing evidence the better." He turned and started up the back stairs to the room he was staying in. "I am going to sleep. Good night, Raven."

Raven watched as Robert walked up the stairs. "Good night, Robert," he replied, with a tinge of sadness to his voice.

# Chapter One

David Masterson listened to the sounds of early morning traffic as he walked to his first class of the day. In his backpack was the final sketches he made for his portraiture final project. His friend, Ben had been gracious enough to pose for him for three hours last night as David sketched. His pencil rubbing, his thumb smudging, Ben had sat perfectly still, even though David knew the position he was in couldn't possibly be comfortable. Now it was done and David looked forward to being out of this class and moving on. David despised sketches, his real passion was paint. He loved the feel and the smell of the paint. He loved the imperfections created by the brush strokes, tiny stray bristles that sometimes make minute marks. Imperfections, just like life

As he thought about painting he wondered if he could get Ben to pose again so he could paint him. David smiled at the thought of his friend, helping him once again. Ben was a great model, cooperative, and had good bone structure.

David was a first year Visual Arts student at the University of Windsor when he met Ben Steele. Now in his second year, he spent most of his free time with Ben and their friends. But he held a special place in his heart for Ben. There was a trust there that no matter what he did, Ben wouldn't judge him in any way at all. Then of course there was the best part, Ben, like all of their other friends, was a Christian.

David had been following Christ for some time when he met Ben. At the time Ben had just been pulled out of a demon worshiping cult, and was struggling to kick a drug habit. With the help of their friends, and Christ, he succeeded. David felt that a special kind of bond had been created as the small group of students watched over and helped Ben through the withdrawal symptoms that had racked his body. The endless nights of fevers and the seemingly unending string of curses and insults that issued from Ben's mouth, which would then quickly turned to tears and depression. This had somehow created a bond that brought David and Ben closer than any conventional friendship could ever achieve. David found great pleasure in watching Ben find the Lord after that. He thought of it as seeing the birth of a new child, and in a way it was.

David ran his fingers through his long blond hair and pulled his backpack closer to his short, stocky body. Despite his gentle appearance, his powerful limbs held a strength that would surprise any who saw him. Years of working in a grain mill on the outskirts of a small Amish community called Elmira, worked his muscles to tight, powerful arms and legs. For hours he would throw bag upon bag of feed for different animals onto a truck, or offload bins of grain to the work floor.

Right now his thoughts drifted to another member of their group and a troubling conversation that he had with her. David told Marianne the night before that he loved her and that one day, if the Lord allowed, he wanted to marry her. Marianne's reaction was not bad, but it also gave David doubts. Doubts about himself and doubts about a feeling that he believed was from God. From the first moment he met her, David was sure that Marianne was the woman he would spend the rest of his life with. The feeling was so intense and he was so sure, that it could only have come from the Lord Himself. That was what David thought anyway. Now he was starting to doubt that.

As he passed the old Assumption church, with its tall spires reaching upward and scratching at the blue sky, he was surprised to see police vehicles and an ambulance parked on the grass of the Victorian building, their lights flashing in the early sun. People moved in and out of the brass front doors and an older priest was crying off to the side, he was being comforted by a uniformed officer, with her arm around his shoulder. David stopped and joined the already growing crowd. He said a silent prayer that no one was badly injured or, if they were, that Jesus would keep them safe. He glanced around and noticed that there were many small groups of students and police officers standing around just talking. The excitement must have been over, no one was in a hurry.

Suddenly, the crowd hissed in excitement and the newspaper photographers clicked their cameras, David's eyes widened in horror as a stretcher was pulled out of the church and brought to the ambulance. The sheet was coated in a thick layer of blood that had seeped through the coarse fabric, and as the attendant lifted it to the waiting ambulance one of the hands fell out, but was quickly placed back under the sheet by a police officer. David quickly turned his head and started toward the cafeteria to meet his small group of friends.

David moved woodenly for a few steps his feet seemingly not under his control and jerking spasmodically. He struggled to concentrate on the impossible task of walking, then started into a light jog to meet the others for their daily breakfast bible study. He forced himself to hold back the tears that were gathering near the edges of his eyes. The image in his mind was all that he saw, though as he leapt the stairs, nearly knocking over a few people who turned around and growled obscenities at his retreating form. He burst through the cafeteria doors and winced at the bang they made as they crashed against the wall. He walked through the doors into the cafeteria, gulping deep breaths of air to try to slow his heart. Scanning the room slowly through tear filled eyes he saw the table with his friends; he forced himself to walk calmly, dodging the occasional student, and made his way to the table where the others were sitting.

As he took his customary seat beside Marianne Storm he began to cry softly at the image burned into his mind. His shoulders shook gently and he let his backpack slide to the floor with a thud. The sight was still there and he couldn't make it leave, as if it was burned into the backs of his eyelids, even when he closed them, the image remained.

Marianne leaned over to lay a hand gently on David's shoulder. David had loved Marianne romantically for some time and normally took great comfort in her touch, relishing every hug and touch. Today it seemed cold, and uncaring, and he pulled sharply away from her, with a sharp hiss.

Marianne turned her bright, blue eyes to the others and brushed her long, blond hair away from her face, curling it behind one ear. She tried to look down at David, but he had covered his face with his hands.

Michael Mclester sat opposite Marianne and sadly shook his normally happy chubby cheeks in confusion. His face was broad and generally a rosy red, looking somewhat like Santa Clause would have looked if he were twenty one years old. A disheveled mop of brown hair sat on his head and frequently fell into his deep, brown eyes, brushing a lock out of the way, he shrugged his shoulders helplessly.

"David, whenever you're ready to talk, we're here for you," he said, his voice gentle and soothing.. David nodded quickly in reply, simply trying to force his heart to stop pounding, with every beat the image in his mind pulsed, with greater focus, greater detail.

Across from Mike sat Sara Blanchard, she silently closed her big brown eyes and prayed for knowledge and wisdom of how to handle David's problem, whatever it may be. Curly brown hair framed her delicate face and waved gently as she spoke to Jesus in hushed tones.

Beside Sara sat Ben Steele. He rubbed a hand over his black hair that fell around his shoulders in ringlets, and turned slate blue eyes to David, examining him. A short, neatly trimmed beard grew on his chin and he rubbed it softly as he studied David for a moment before smiling.

"David," Ben said casually. "Did I forget to put the top on the toothpaste again?" David looked up at his friend, suddenly his eyes wide and shocked. Ben, David and Mike shared a house together and the toothpaste was a pet peeve of David's that Ben always seemed to get involved in.

"No, Mike used it last," David said with a weak smile. He took a deep breath and exhaled slowly before he looked up and met Ben's face. He found a calm comfort in Ben's eyes, almost the kind of comfort he felt when he was alone and speaking with Jesus. "I was just walking here, past the old Catholic church. Something happened there last night. There was police and newspapers and it was a madhouse! Then they brought out a body on a stretcher. He was dead. The sheet was covered in blood," David's voice started to quiver, rising to an almost hysterical pitch. He stopped, holding back tears. Marianne reached out and touched his shoulder again. David didn't pull back this time and drew strength from the touch of a loved friend. "Then his hand fell out from under the sheet," he continued, his voice suddenly softer, so much so that the others had to lean in to hear him. "There was a nail driven through it, at the wrist." The image was there for a brief moment, curling claw-like fingers, the nail driven deep through the wrist. Dried blood coated everything, hanging from the fingernails and knuckles, like red sap.

Then David broke down and let the tears come freely. Marianne held him tightly and prayed softly for comfort. She rocked him softly back and forth, as he cried into her shoulder.

Sara opened her eyes and shivered. "I have a feeling that this has something to do with the Occult," she said. "I don't know why, but it's so strong in my heart right now." Her gaze immediately went to Ben, knowing his past, and fearing his reaction.

Ben's eyes narrowed and he inhaled sharply, fighting the urge to bore down on Sara with a cold glare. He stared at the table instead, willing it to burst into flames just with the fire in his eyes.

Mike looked at Sara in surprise and said, "Then we should find out more about this. We've been ordered by God to battle Satan wherever we find him." He leaned in, conspiratorial.

Marianne nodded as well. "Yes, I feel it too."

David looked up, hope in his face for the first time since he arrived. "That might be a good idea," he said weakly. "I have to be able to feel good about this. I have to know that God is in control of that church."

"Let the police deal with this," Ben said, his voice a deep bass rumble, deep in his chest. He wasn't looking at any of them, merely staring at the tabletop.

David stared at his friend. Ben's voice got softer as he got angrier, and now it was just barely a whisper, David had to struggle to hear him.

"Ben, we've been ordered by the Lord to combat Satan and his forces, wherever we find him," Marianne said.

"The police are the people to handle this situation," Ben whispered. His hands were clenched tightly into fists under the table and shaking with the strain. “Our battle is not against flesh and blood.”

David placed a restraining hand on Marianne’s arm when she started to talk. "Ben why don't we just look and see what this is about?" he said, wiping the tears from his eyes. "Then we can figure out if this is something that has to do with the Occult or not," he said.

Sara looked at Ben intently with care in her eyes and said, "Ben, I don't know if you're afraid, but you don't have to be because God is bigger than any daemon we could find. It'll be OK."

Ben whipped his hands up and smashed them down onto the table, rattling the dishes and causing the nearby conversations to stop for a moment. "I'm not afraid for me," he hissed in silent anger. "I've been through it once. I'm afraid for all of you."

Marianne leaned over and took Ben's hand softly in hers. "God will take care of us."

Ben looked up and caught Marianne's gaze with his ice blue eyes, drilling into her the seriousness of his words. "I know that. But there are things involved in the Occult that will challenge your faith in God and in Jesus. It will make you wish we hadn't started this entire thing." He took his hand away from Marianne and pointed at everyone in the group. "I want you all to know, before we start poking around in this just how seriously we'd be involved." Then he looked at David, a stern expression on his face. "We aren't talking about a kid messing around with a Ouija board. We're talking about a guy who's so far into it that he's willing to kill."

The small group looked around at each other. Fear traced their faces as they thought about this new idea that Ben had given them. Then David closed his eyes, and took a deep breath, held it, then let it out slowly.

"I still feel that we have to find out if this has anything to do with the Occult," he said firmly. “And if it does, we have to help stop it. I'm not talking about going out and catching the guy ourselves. I'm just saying that we should look into it and help, if we can."

Ben looked down at his lap and sighed softly. "I knew this guy; his name was Greg, he was in the same cult as me. His father was a pastor and he tried to get Greg out. He was bringing lawsuits against the cult leaders and all kinds of stuff. But Greg was over eighteen and there was nothing really that his Dad could do." Ben lifted his face and locked eyes with David. "I remember he left the meeting house late one night after speaking with the leader and then he came back again about two hours later." He paused, watching David's face for a moment, scanning his eyes. The table was silent, and the silence was deafening.

"What happened?" Mike asked softly, daring to break the tension Ben had created.

Ben's eyes never left David's. "The police found the pastor's body torn to shreds by a wood chipper in the county. They had to identify him with DNA."

David's eyes closed and tears started to form at the lids again. He quickly wiped them away and took a deep breath.

"I don't want to make you upset, David," Ben said his voice now soft, genuinely caring for his distraught friend. "I just want you to know the situation."

"I know the risks now and I'm scared," David said. Then he added firmly. "But I will not be scared off by Satan or his daemons."

Ben looked at each face in turn and they nodded their agreement to what David said. Then he abruptly stood and picked up his tray. The others watched in surprise as he slowly, and quietly walked to the far wall of the cafeteria and placed his tray on a rack with the other dirty dishes. He stood there for a moment, head bowed, thinking about his friends, and praying for guidance and wisdom on the decision they were about to make. He turned and walked back to the table and stood before the small group in silence for a moment. David started to say something, but was quickly silenced by a raised finger from Ben.

"Marianne, Sara and Mike. Why don't you guys go to the Library and find out what cults have a beef with the Catholic church. David and I will go to the church and snoop around there," Ben said suddenly.

They all looked at Ben in amazement for a moment, and then Marianne said, "You're going to help then?"

"Did you think I was going to let you bumble around by yourselves?" Ben smiled weakly.

# Chapter Two

The Leddy Building was the University of Windsor's large, four story world class library. It was divided into two different wings and held a cornucopia of information on a wide range of subjects, as is expected in most universities. The entire holding of the library had been put onto a computer system and all one had to do was type in a subject, and the computer would direct you to the appropriate area complete with a map on the screen to show you how to get to the appropriate stack.. When Sara, Marianne and Mike arrived they found very little having to do with the Occult.

"There's not much to go on," Mike said as he peered dejectedly at the computer screen. He clicked the mouse a few more times, looking for another subject that could be tied into the Occult, but he found that was lacking as well.

"Well, let's just go to the section and maybe we'll find something we can use there," Marianne said. “God might lead us to the right book.”

They took the elevator to the second level where the books on Occultism were kept. From there they delegated who was going to be looking through which areas of the shelves. Marianne split up the workload so that each person was going to be looking through about twenty books.

As the afternoon wore on, Sara sat down beside Marianne at the table where they had piled loads of books. She glanced out of the corner of her eyes at the blond haired girl and sighed. Then she looked down at the book, a concerned look on her face.

"Marianne?" Sara said softly.

"Yes, Sweety?" Marianne replied, not looking up from the book she was reading.

"What are your feelings for David?"

"I love him."

"You know what I mean."

Marianne looked up and sat back in her chair. "I..." she started and then her face scrunched up in an oddly confused expression, "I don't know." She took a deep breath and let it out slowly, through puffed out cheeks.

"What do you think you feel for him?" Sara asked.

"I've always wanted someone to love me the way that he says he does," Marianne continued. "He said that he'd wait for me and that he would always love me. He loves me unconditionally, he doesn't demand anything from me, and all he wants to do is give me his love."

"But what do you feel for him?" Sara said again, stressing the word "you". "David told me a few days ago he told you that, and I was just wondering what you felt for him." She looked up at Marianne and suddenly blushed a little. "If you don't want to tell me then you don't have to."

"I really don't know, Sara," Marianne replied. "And don't worry. You're my best friend and I'll tell you anything," she added, taking Sara's small hand in hers, squeezing it, then letting it go.

"Have you prayed about it?"

"Yes, of course I have. I've asked for a sign," Marianne said as she looked back at the book.

Sara glanced at her book for a moment then looked up again.

"What kind of sign?" she asked.

Marianne shook her head. "It's not that I don't trust you Sara," she said. "But I want to make sure that the sign comes from God and no one else."

Sara opened another book and scanned the table of contents. "I'm just worried about David's feelings," she said.

"I know, Sara. So am I. The last thing I want to do is hurt him," Marianne replied. "Which, I suppose, is an indicator of my feelings for him as well."

They sat in the library for most of the afternoon, looking through the library books for clues as to what cult had a problem with the Catholic religion. They're eyes began to dry out and every once in a while they had to stand, just to stretch their legs.

At one point, Sara stood and stretched her arms, then she slowly made her way to the high shelves they had been taking their books from. Reaching out to grab a book, she was suddenly startled when someone dropped a thick book onto the floor beside her.

"I'm terribly sorry," said a thin man. Sara had not noticed him before. "I didn't mean to startle you." His voice was soft and carried a slight English accent, perhaps Welsh.

Sara smiled, taking note that the man dressed all in black and sported a long, black ponytail. He wore a long black leather coat. "That's perfectly all right," she said, pulling the book she wanted from the shelf.

The man glanced over Sara's shoulder and noted the title of the book in her hands. "Demonology in History," he said. "Are you interested in Demonology?"

Sara smiled cordially and said, "No, we're just doing some research on the Occult."

The man in black scanned Sara's face intently for a moment then smiled. "Are you with the police?" he asked. "Last night there was a horrible murder in the church."

Sara laughed and shook her head. "Oh, no, we're just looking into it because we believe that it's the right thing to do."

The man nodded and placed his finger on his lip. His nail was immaculately manicured and long.

"You must be Christian," he stated after a moment of scratching his lip in thought.

Sara nodded and held her hand out to the man. "Yes, I'm a Born Again Christian. My name's Sara."

The man took Sara's hand delicately and held it in his hand as he said, "A pleasure to meet you, Sara. I am called Raven."

Sara smiled, "That's an interesting name."

"I have an interesting family," Raven said. Then his eyes scanned the titles on the shelf beside them. "This may help you." He released Sara's hand and pulled a book from the shelf with his manicured hands, handing it to her.

Sara looked down at the title and smiled. "Thank you very much." Raven returned the smile and picked up the book he had dropped.

"The pleasure's all mine, my dear," he said before he turned and walked back up the aisle.

Sara returned to the table and placed both books' in front of her.

She stared intently at the one Raven had given her, and then she opened the cover and looked through the table of contents.

Her eyes scanned the page quickly, looking for any sign of Demonology with the Catholic religion. Then her eyes caught on one chapter. 'The Catholics and Nigorsus'

She quickly turned to that chapter and scanned it over. "I've found something!" she exclaimed.

Marianne and Mike went and looked over Sara's shoulder as she said, "It looks like the Catholic Church tried to eliminate the cult of Nigorsus about five hundred years ago. It didn't work out and the cult survived, just barely. There have been acts of vengeance going on by the cult ever since. This may be one of them."

"Good work!" Mike said as he quickly hugged Sara.

"It wasn't me, it was God. There was a strange man who helped me find this book. He was dressed all in black and had an English accent," Sara explained.

Marianne looked worried. "Are you sure he was there to help us?"

Sara nodded. "Yes, I am. Besides, how would he have known to be here? We just started working on this today."

"Satan moves his pieces just like God does," Marianne said as she sat down again.

Mike smiled at the two of them and said, "Why don't you copy some of that stuff out and Marianne and I will finish going through the last of these books, just in case there are any other little cults that may be suspects," Mike said.

"I feel good about this, Mike," Sara said.

Mike nodded. "So do I, but we should still be sure."

Sara started to photocopy some of the pages in the book and Mike and Marianne scanned their way through the last few texts they had to go through. They found no other cults that could be linked to any violent acts against the Catholic Church, so they left the library a little happier than they had arrived and started back to Mike's house.

Raven walked into his house and placed the book he borrowed from the Leddy library on his coffee table. Robert was sitting on the couch with a tea and looking through a large leather bound tome on his lap.

"How old is this?" Robert asked Raven, conversationally.

Raven shrugged off his coat and placed it on a coat rack by the door. "About two hundred years," he said. "There were some students at the library, looking up some information on Demonic cults."

Robert nodded and sipped quietly at his tea. He turned a page of the book and muttered, "Go on."

"They seem to think that it has something to do with last night," Raven said, sitting in his chair.

Robert looked up and leaned back into the couch, inhaling deeply and enjoying the scented incense that floated through the air from a demon shaped holder on the coffee table.

"What happened?" Robert asked.

"I gave them information leading to the cult of Nigorsus," Raven forced a smile.

Robert smiled and then let out a short laugh. "That cult is all but dead!"

Raven stood and started into the kitchen. "And it soon will be dead," he muttered, but his heart wasn't with the words.

# Chapter Three

Assumption Catholic Church is one of the oldest churches in Windsor. The parish was placed under the guidance of the Basilian Fathers since 1870, and before that, in the summer of 1728, Father Armand De La Richardie, came from Quebec to establish a mission among the Huron Indians. It was given the imposing title of “The Mission of Our Lady of the Assumption among the Hurons of Detroit.”. Now, it provided an imposing scene as the two students approached its large brass doors. Police still walked into and out of the church and as the two young men got to the door a uniformed officer stopped them just short of a yellow strip of plastic.

"May I help you?" he asked politely.

"Yes, we're doing an investigation of the Occult in Windsor and we wondered if we may be permitted to ask some questions of the officer in charge. We have some reason to believe that this may, in some way be connected with the Occult," Ben said smoothly.

The officer looked the two students up and down before asking, "What kind of 'investigation' is this?"

"It involves a paper I'm planning to write on the Occult," Ben replied. "I'm an ancient religions student at the school of religion here at the University."

The officer thought for a moment and then said, "Stay here, I'll go ask the officer in charge if he has time for you." He turned on his heel and entered the church.

"You lied!" David suddenly accused his friend.

"About what?" Ben replied calmly.

"You said we were doing an investigation."

"We are. We're investigating whether or not this has Occult properties."

"You also told him you were planning on writing a paper on the Occult."

"I will... someday," Ben smiled. "I'm sure at some point I'll have to write a paper on the Occult."

David seemed at a loss for words and looked around for something else to charge Ben with, and then suddenly he shook his head in disbelief and laughed. A moment later the officer came back outside.

"He says you can come in for a little while, as long as he can ask you a few questions," he said. "But don't touch anything or walk anywhere without and officer with you."

Ben nodded, "No problem."

David looked a bit nervous. Ben shot him and confident grin and nodded slightly. David had always envied Ben his confidence and easy going attitude. David spent much of his time worrying. Worrying about school, or his friendships, and lately worrying about Marrianne.

The two men entered the church and could smell the old dust and wood of many years past. the vast sanctuary was quiet, with the exception of the footsteps of the officers and the low mumbling of the forensics experts dusting the area.

A bloodied cross was standing at the foot of the aisle they used and a light outline on the left wall gave testimony as to where it had once stood. On the floor sat the broken remains of a statue of Jesus with his arms outstretched. Obviously the statue had been on the cross, before it was replaced.

David stumbled as he saw the blood that was still on the floor and quickly grabbed Ben's shoulder to stay upright. As Ben held onto David's arm he pointed at the far right wall; written in blood were the words, "TALUBSI! ADULA! ULU! BAACHUR!"

A large man with a huge barrel chest and thick tree, trunk arms walked up to them and shook each hand in turn saying, "Hello I'm Detective Greg Martin. I here you guys are into this Occult garbage."

David shrugged his shoulders, "Well, kind of, we're Christians but my friend here is going to write a paper on occult activities, so we came here." he said with a shy smile, not meeting the detective's eyes. "I'm David Masterson, and this is Ben Steele." Martin shook each man's hand again.

Ben smiled at how easily David fell into the "investigator" role, and was impressed with how he had come out of his shell to start talking. As David talked with the detective he wandered casually over to the writing and stood before it, praying silently.

"Well," Martin continued, "We obviously have Occult activity in this situation. The deceased was nailed to the cross after the attacker removed the statue. The priest was dead before he was nailed on, small mercy, I guess," he said with a shrug. He pointed to where Ben was standing. "We also found a bowl with burnt hair and other assorted herbs mixed in, just under that writing. Forensics will break it down for us."

David followed the big man over to where Ben was intently looking at the bloodied writing on the wall. On the floor, blood had dripped from the writing into a small pool, the smell of burnt hair was still in the air.

"Was this all the stuff that you found?" Ben asked.

"Yep, and that leaves a lot of unanswered questions," Martin replied.

"Like what?" David asked.

"Like the fact that the little stage over there where the priest conducts mass has been totally emptied. You can see it. The communion table is neatly pushed over to one side and the chairs are pushed over to the other side. Why? There's also some weird discolouration on the floor up there. Like a big circle was drawn," Martin said as he led Ben and David to the front of the church.

Ben frowned in thought as he looked at the floor, he knelt and touched the darkened area that made the outline of a circle on the floor. There was a dark discolouration on the floor, roughly five metres in diameter. He scrubbed at the discolouration with a finger and brought them to his nose.

"What is it, Ben?" David asked.

"Coal, earth," he mumbled.

"What have you found?" Martin said, quickly leaning down with Ben..

"Someone has tampered with your crime scene, Detective," Ben said.

"Call me Martin, and what are you talking about?"

"This circle is made out of coal. That's normally used as the element, earth in summoning rituals," Ben explained.

"Hold on! You're moving too fast for me," Martin said as he put up his hands in confusion. "What do you mean a summoning ritual? As in B-grade horror movies?"

"I wish it was as simple as a horror movie. I mean like someone came in here meaning to summon something but then had to clean up quickly," Ben replied. Then he noticed that Martin and David were both looking blankly at him "OK, I'll explain in detail. You can't summon anything without having a circle with which to contain the being summoned. That circle has to be made out of the five elements."

"Wait a second, I know this. There's only four elements," David said.

Martin looked at David. "I thought you were an expert in this too?" he asked.

David shook his head. "I'm an expert in the Christian part. He's the Occult guy. He's working on a degree in ancient religions," he said shooting a thumb at Ben.

Ben smiled, and then continued, "When you're dealing with the Occult, David, you need five elements. We all know the first four, earth, fire, water, and air. The fifth is the void. That represents the powers that are drawn on to summon the daemon. Magick," Ben said. "Magick spelled m-a-g-i-c-k. The other kind is just that slight of hand stuff."

"Are you trying to tell me that someone tried to summon a daemon in a

Catholic church?" Martin asked hotly. “Listen, I'm just looking for a murderer. I didn't sign up for daemons and magick with a “k”.”

"Yes, that's exactly what I'm saying," Ben replied. "You don't believe in any of this stuff do you?" He said after a quick examination of Martin.

David turned to look at Martin to hear the response.

Martin faltered for a moment before answering. "Well, I believe in God and all, but as for daemons and Magick and all that stuff, I mean that's just too weird," he answered. "And what's with this Magick with a 'k'?"

"Magic without the 'k' refers to slight of hand, like card tricks and stuff. Sawing a woman in half for example," Ben explained. "Anton Levay, the guy who wrote the 'Satanic Bible,' coined the term Magick with the 'k,' that refers to the powers that were used here."

Martin shook his head and rubbed his eyes, mumbling under his breath. He raised a shaky hand and rubbed his forehead. He suddenly looked like a deer in the headlights.

Ben took Martin by the shoulder and locked his blue eyes with Martin's brown ones saying, "You're dealing with forces that you don't understand and have no defense from. These people are willing to kill for what they believe in. I'm not even sure you know what to believe in. I'm here to tell you that this is real, I've seen it and I've been a part of it. Then Jesus saved me and freed me from all that." Then Ben took a step forward and pointed at the cross. "If you don't decide what you believe in and get too close to these people you'll end up like that priest. These are bad people that do bad things because something tells them to."

“This is insane,” Martin muttered, “Magick and demons and circles. People summoning demons in churches!” He paused for a minute then asked, "What do you believe in?" to David.

"I believe that the only way to walk is with Jesus, hand in hand," David replied without pause.

Martin turned and walked over to the writing on the wall, a thoughtful expression on his face.

"Where do you think he stands?" Ben asked David.

"I think he's a fence sitter at best," David said. "But we've got him thinking at least."

"Ben! David!" Martin called from the far wall. The two young men walked over to the large, burly officer and looked at him quizzically.

"Why would the killers clean up that circle but not this?", the big man asked. "And what is this?"

"This is like a ritual to get help, or an answer from a daemon. The hair in the bowl would be an important part of the evocation. I'm willing to bet that it's the hair of the priest," Ben replied. "It's an old ritual that involves a human sacrifice. I've never even heard of it being used for the last two hundred years or so."

An officer came and whispered something in Martin's ear. After a moment Martin turned to the friends and said, "I've got to go for a few minutes I'll be right back. Don't touch anything."

Ben and David said they'd wait and after Martin left an older priest came up to them and pulled them into a small alcove in the sanctuary. David recognized him as the priest that was crying when he walked by the church this morning.

"You are involved with the investigation?" he asked in an old raspy voice.

"I wouldn't say we're involved, but yes, we're helping to answer some questions with it," David said carefully.

"I overheard that you're Christians?" the priest said. Ben and David nodded, confused.

"Because of my vows I can't tell you who or the exact nature of his sin but I can tell you this. My advice to him was '1 Corinthians 10:20,21,' that is all 1 can tell you, please don't ask for more." The priest then turned and slowly shuffled out of the sanctuary.

After he had left David turned to Ben with a bewildered look and said,

"That was ... interesting."

Ben looked at David with a blank expression and replied, "Yes." He then he shook his head. "OK, do you have your Bible with you?"

David shot Ben an, 'Are you an idiot?' look and dug into his pocket pulling out a small Bible. He quickly opened it and a wad of notes and pieces of folded paper came tumbling out. Ben smiled as he knelt to pick them up and told David to find the scripture.

"Here it is," David said. "No, but the sacrifice of pagans is offered to daemons, not to God, and I do not want you to be participants with daemons. You cannot drink of the cup of the Lord and the cup of daemons too; You cannot have part in both the Lord's table and the table of daemons." David closed his Bible. "I wonder who he said that to?"

"I don't know but I bet it has something to do with last night," Ben replied. He glanced down at David's papers and saw a poem in David's handwriting. The title read, 'To Marianne.' David quickly took the papers with a shy look on his face.

"What does?" Martin said as he walked up from behind them. Ben and David told Martin about the scripture. After they finished telling him, Martin sat in one of the pews rubbing his temples.

"This feels like an episode of the Twilight Zone," Martin said. "First I get a call, a dead priest, OK, I can handle dead priests, rotten thing to do, but I can deal with it. Then I get here and see that writing on the wall, I get a little freaked out now, some really weird lunatic, I say. Then you two come along and tell me that someone tried to raise a daemon in the sanctuary of a flipping Catholic church, and that if I don't become a born again Christian that I'm going to end up on this weirdo's ten most wanted list! That's when I start saying to myself that this is getting really strange and I might just want to think about retiring. Now I find out that there's a priest running around giving out Bible verses that he says is important to my case. This is just too strange for me. But you know what?" Martin stood slowly back to his feet an almost insane grin on his face. "I'm going to stick with it, just so I can shoot this little jerk, whoever he is, for making my life a loony bin in one day!" He stood, took a deep, calming breath and turned back. "Let's trade numbers so we can keep in touch if we need to," he said in a more normal tone.

They traded numbers and Ben asked if they could look around a little bit more. Martin said it wouldn't be a problem as long as they didn't move or touch anything.

Ben and David left shortly after Martin, finding nothing more interesting. They returned to the Victorian style house they shared with Mike and, Ben made himself a cup of Earl Grey tea and sat in his favourite paisley, plush chair. David sat on the couch and tried to concentrate on reading an article about modern art. There they sat in the living room in silence for a moment before David said, "I wonder if that's what Christ's cross looked like after they took Him off it."

Ben looked up from the magazine he was looking at. "I guess that's probably what it looked like. The priest was killed in the same way."

"There was a lot of blood," David said in a hollow tone.

"You OK, David?" Ben said as he put the magazine down. Ben had lived in a violent subculture, where people were beaten, and hurt in painful and imaginative ways. He needed to remember that this was all new to David.

"Yeah, it's just that I've never seen so much blood before." David stretched out on the couch and prayed softly to himself.

Ben had to smile to himself as he watched David's face relax. He lifted the magazine again and flipped through it until he found an article that looked interesting. He read it for a moment then looked down at his friend that was lying in silence on the couch.

"I love her," David said suddenly, rolling to face Ben.

"I know, David," Ben smiled, glancing over the magazine to his friend. "Feels good doesn't it?"

"I'll wait as long as it takes. I told her that. The only way I'll give up is if she marries another man."

"Just watch out for yourself too," Ben said, laying the magazine down on his lap.

David laid back on the couch. "I just want to make Marianne happy," he said before closing his eyes and falling asleep. Ben whispered a short prayer for his friend, then went back to his article.

A few hours later Marianne, Mike and Sara came into the house. They apologized to David as he slowly sat up and rubbed his eyes. They quickly shared the information they found at the library but a quick look from Sara prevented Mike or Marianne from telling Ben and David about her encounter with Raven. Then Ben and David related their experiences.

"That is so neat!" Marianne said when David told them about the Priest and the scripture. "I wonder what it means."

"We may never find out," Ben said. "We don't know if Martin will call us again or not. We can call him tomorrow and give him the information you guys found at Leddy, then we have to wait until he calls us."

David looked over from where he was starting a fire in the large brick fireplace. "I think there's more to this than just a cult trying to get revenge for something that happened five hundred years ago," he said. Once the fire was lit he went back to the couch.

"I think we should all remember to pray for protection for each other tonight," Mike called from the kitchen, where he was fixing dinner.

Marianne went to the kitchen to get a can of Coke. "I like that idea," she called.

"And don't forget Martin," David said. "He's not saved."

Marianne came back from the kitchen and sat down on the floor in front of David. She took a long drink of her Coke then put it on the floor beside her. David looked down and began to slowly brush her hair with his fingers. Marianne leaned back and closed her eyes.

"It's nice that we can get together and relax, knowing that God will keep us safe from harm. Even with all the spiritual warfare going on," Marianne said.

Sara had sat down on the arm of the chair Ben was sitting in. He leaned back and put his head on Sara's shoulder, relaxing seemed like a good thing right now. He had been thinking about daemons and magickal circles all day and right now he just wanted to sit back and relax with Sara. He looked over to where David was sitting with Marianne.

David softly pulled his fingers through Marianne's long blond hair. He really did love her and it was times like this when he wished the world would stop and God would let him spend eternity here. He felt Ben looking at him and looked up and smiled shyly at his friend. Ben knew how he felt because Ben felt the same way for Sara. The only difference was that Sara returned those feelings back to Ben.

Secretly Ben looked at this situation as a blessing and a curse. It was a blessing because he could look at David's situation and see just how precious his was with Sara. However he could also look at it and try to understand the pain that David was in whenever the topic came up that Marianne didn't return those feelings. Ben secretly thought it was a cruel cosmic joke that someone was playing on David.

Mike walked out of the kitchen with a platter of steaming nachos. The cheese was melted evenly over them and he carried another tray with various types of sauces to dip them in.

"Dinner's ready!" he smiled.

"Looks good, Mike," David said, somewhat sadly, but only Ben noticed.

The small group gathered around the coffee table and made short work of Mike's feast. They talked and laughed, none of them talking about the death of the priest, or the information that they had gathered about the cults. When the last of the nachos were eaten and Mike was complaining about a sore stomach from laughing so much, Ben and Sara went into the kitchen and did the dishes. When they came back out Ben watched as David said very little to anyone. He watched as David grew more and more distant and the silence grew more and more thick.

His friend was retreating into himself. Ben had seen it many times, it was a common tactic that cults used to alienate people from their non-cult families and friends. A person would be brought into the cult and then slowly forced to retreat from society. Not calling family or friends, not going outside the confines of the cults influence.

David's case was obviously different, but Ben was sure it would end the same way. David, alienating himself from the small group that they had.

The phone rang and David leaned over grabbing it from where he sat on the couch.

"Hello," he said into the receiver.

"Hi, this is Martin, from the church this afternoon," was the reply.

"Hi, Martin. We were just going to call you tomorrow morning."

David quickly related to the Detective what they had learned from the library. After he finished he asked, "So you called us, what was it you wanted?"

"I'd like for you and Ben to meet me at the church in fifteen," Marting said, then he added, "We just got some new information and I wanted your input."

"Sure no problem," David said, then he hung up the phone.

David told the others what Martin said and Ben frowned in thought for a moment, leaning against the wall, his arms crossed over his chest.

"I wonder what that's all about," he mused. "He didn't say anything else?"

"Nope, just that he wanted to see us at the church," David said. "He sounded pretty urgent about it."

"Maybe he wants to commit himself to God," Marianne said with a smile. Ben had his brow furrowed in thought then suddenly looked up and smiled at Marianne.

"As great as that would be, I don't think it's that good." Then he smiled cryptically for a moment. "I think it has something to do with the fact that there were two cults involved in last night's little shindig at the church."

"Two? How did you come to that conclusion, Sherlock?" David asked.

"Elementary really, Watson," Ben smiled. "as long as you know about the Occult. You look at the two things that were going on; the circle and the small ritual by the wall were totally inconsistent. They have no relation whatsoever so why would they be in the same place at the same time, let alone in a church? Therefore we can assume that they were two totally different ceremonies." Ben smiled. "I'm willing to bet that the smaller ritual was performed by the killer and the circle was drawn by someone who has access to the church at all hours." Ben got up and put his coat on.

"I think we've created a monster," David laughed.

"Well, Watson," Ben said to David, with a horrible fake English accent. "Ready to go find out what the good detective wants?"

"Guys," Sara said. "This isn't a joke ... be careful." She got up and gave David a hug and then went to Ben. "And you don't take any chances, OK?" she said as she gave Ben a soft kiss.

Ben smiled broadly. "Hey! It's me!"

"That's what we're all worried about, Ben," Marianne said with a chuckle.

# Chapter Four

The wind was cold and bit through Ben and David's coats as they made their way to the church. They walked in silence, the thought that Sara had planted in their heads was blooming now into actual fear. This wasn't a joke, or a game, they both knew that. But there was a small part of Ben that thought as long as he thought of it as a game of some kind, then he wouldn't be scared. The memory of the blood on the cross came unbidden to his head, people had died. This wasn't a game. More thoughts went through his head like grains of sand in an hourglass, each thought making way for another to bloom.

When they reached the church the feeling of excitement was gone. It was no longer Sherlock and Watson, it was two frightened university students, standing in the light of an old Catholic church, waiting to talk to a police detective about a murder.

The officer on duty asked to see some identification, and after checking it he mentioned that Detective Martin had radioed ahead and given clearance for them to go in and wait for him. The door was unlocked, so they walked in and waited in the back pew. The cross still stood at the front of the church, the dried blood looking like rust on the crooked wooden cross.

Suddenly the front door slammed shut and both young men jumped and turned to see Martin walking toward them.

"Hello, guys," he said.

"Hi, Martin," Ben said trying to catch his breath.

"Hello, Martin," David said, closing his eyes and trying to slow his heart down.

"Sorry if I startled you," Martin smiled, talking softer to try to prevent the echo his full voice caused. "I wouldn't want to spend any time in here alone either." He sat down in the pew in front of them and turned to face the students.

“We’re never really alone,” Ben said with a smile.

"So, what's up?" David asked, shooting a grin at Ben.

"We've got a problem here guys," Martin said switching to a more business-like tone. "The forensics guys found a box full of stuff jammed under the pulpit."

"What kind of stuff?" Ben asked.

"I was just getting to that," Martin smiled. "The box had a lump of charcoal, a wad of incense, an incense holder, an empty wooden bowl, six candles and a jar of what looks like ebony." Martin paused for a moment. "They also found an ornate knife with traces of blood on it." He paused and raised his eyebrows at his audience. "That's not the best part though. We found some pretty clear fingerprints and they belong to the dead priest."

"So? What's the problem? The priest cleaned up the circle, one mystery solved," Ben said.

"No, it's not that easy. Some of the prints were weeks, even months old," Martin replied with a stern face. “They were layered over and over, took a pretty powerful computer quite a while to make sense of them.”

"Wait a second," David interrupted. "Are you saying that the priest had something to do with the circle that was drawn?"

"It looks that way. Strike one for religious faith," Martin said. “Coroner also said there were traces of charcoal stained into the skin of the priest’s hands.”

"That's disgusting!" David spat the words out like they were a bad taste in his mouth.

"The Scripture," Ben whispered.

"What about it?" Martin asked.

"'You can't drink of the cup of the Lord and the cup of daemons.' Yeah, it must have been the dead priest the older priest was talking about," David said. "And please don't base your entire opinion of faith on the misdeeds of one man."

Martin stood up and gave David a smile. "Well, that may be so, but we still have some unanswered questions. Like why was the priest killed? Why was the circle erased? Who killed the priest? And who made the second ritual thing?" Martin looked down at Ben and David and sighed.

"Is there anything else you found out?" David asked.

"Yes, but I have to know first if you are going to help me with this as my official Occult experts. I can't offer you much money, just a consulting fee."

"I thought we already were," David said with a smile.

"So did I." Ben added. "And besides, we're students, any money is good money."

Martin smiled and looked relieved to have any kind of "experts" in the strange case that he had found himself working on.

"Good, there are a couple of things I want you to see." Martin led them to a small alcove area behind the pulpit. He pointed at a small drawing on the wall just a few centimetres over the floor.

"Forensics found this earlier today," Martin said.

Ben peered at the drawing intently. His brow furrowed in thought and he silently asked God for assistance. "I've seen this before. A long time ago, but I just can't quite place it," he mused.

Ben's thought was interrupted by the sound of Martin's phone going off. Martin looked down at it, irritated, and stopped it, then looked at the small screen with a scowl.

"It's the office. Wait here, I'll be right back," Martin said as he stepped to an alcove on the far side of the church.

After Martin left, David looked down at Ben as he examined the small area on the wall with the drawing. A haunted expression ran across his eyes every so often as he thought of a different time, and a different place.

"Ben, are you OK?" David asked.

Ben's eyes didn't leave the small drawing. "I'll... be OK. Just remembering," he replied. "Can you make a sketch of this?"

"I'd rather not but yeah," David said as he pulled out his ever present sketch pad. He began a quick sketch of the intricate symbols.

As David sketched, Ben's mind wandered back to a time buried deep in his memory, a time he had hoped never to think of again.

It was dark in the room. It was dark and cold. They had given him something to drink and it made him feel funny. Ben turned his head and it felt like it wasn't turning, even though the images in his eyes were changing. There were candles all around him, shedding an eerie glow on the walls of the small room he was in.

Ben heard chanting outside the door, what were they saying? He strained his ears to hear.

"TALUBSI! ADULA! ULU! PARABALUABU! BAACHUR!" was chanted over and over, Ben s eyes began to clear and he looked around at the room. He tried to sit up but he found himself tied to the table which held him. Panic wormed its way into his head and he thrashed and thrashed about. Candles fell and rolled on the floor, spreading wax in spider s web fashion, as his legs broke free of their restraints.

He fell to the floor and his vision was focused on the symbols, drawn in chalk on the floor around the platform where he was tied. One symbol seemed to etch itself into his head.

It was the same symbol on the wall he was staring at. But what was it?

"Guys!!" The voice startled Ben back into reality. He wiped a tear away from his eye and turned to see Martin walking toward him and David.

"There's been another murder. Exactly the same only this time it's at a Baptist church," Martin said as he stopped in front of them. "I want you guys to come and take a look at the scene."

Ben and David looked at each other, fear in both their eyes. There was a moment when it seemed like something passed between them, they both felt resolve and strength flow into their muscles, and they turned to Martin and nodded. The three men ran to Martin's unmarked car and raced to the church with the siren on.

"Ben, here's the sketch," David said from the back seat as he handed the small piece of paper to Ben. "I feel dirty now."

"You can take a shower at home," Ben replied with a smile. "Besides, you know where your heart is and so does God."

"That still doesn't change the fact that I feel dirty," David said as he looked at the symbol over Ben's shoulder.

"It should. Whatever power may be in this symbol is powerless against you and me," Ben said with a raise of his eyebrows.

First Baptist Church had stood on the same plot of land for 200 years and it looked like it. The bricks were worn and made by hand by the slaves that crossed the river from Detroit, some hand prints still visible in the old clay. The roof leaked and it needed some new pews, but the people who attended the church were in love with the Lord and worshiped Him with all their heart.

As the small band walked into the church the first thing they noticed was the cross at the front of the sanctuary. The middle aged black pastor was still nailed to it, his naked body looked like it had been dipped in blood, and still dripping to the floor. David quickly turned his head.

Ben stopped and turned to his friend, seeing the sudden paleness in his face. "I think I saw a woman outside crying. Maybe it was the pastor's wife. Why don't you go out and see what you can do for her," he said.

David nodded and quickly walked out of the small church.

"I'm sorry, I didn't think about that," Martin apologized as he and Ben walked up to the wooden cross. "Do you want to wait outside too?"

"No problem," Ben said. "I've seen worse." His eyes were haunted as he looked around the sanctuary. Martin watched him closely, wondering about the young man's story. What had happened to him?

There was no writing on the walls and no circle marking on the floor anywhere. But at the front of the church, behind the pulpit and in front of the baptismal he found the offering dish. In it was burnt incense, some human hair and what looked like blood. Ben's face contorted in thought and he stood and looked at the baptismal curtain.

Ben grabbed the curtain and opened it. One of the officers yelled at him not to touch anything, but then fell silent. Ben gasped and took a step back. On the wall of the baptismal, drawn in still dripping blood was the same symbol that they had seen at Assumption Church. The same one from his memory.

"Martin! I think it's the same guy," Ben called out.

Martin ran over and stood beside Ben, staring at the dripping symbol.

"You think?" Martin said dryly.

David walked out of the church and over to the side of the street. There he sat down and put his head between his legs. Then he vomited, the dinner that Michael made. After he had composed himself, and wiped his mouth, he stood and looked around for the woman Ben mentioned.

"Excuse me. Is there anything I can do to help you?" David said as he walked up to the weeping woman. He thought it sounded like a stupid question but he couldn't think of anything else to say. His head seemed to be full of cotton.

"No, no it's too late. Too late," the woman said between sobs. Her hands covered her face and she was rocking back and forth.

"Do you know what happened in there?" David asked. Why had he asked that, he suddenly wondered.

"Yes, it has been done again. He's done it again, hasn't he?" the woman replied still covering her face and rocking.

"Do you know what's been done?" David was sure that it wasn't him saying the words. It was like he was only a spectator watching what was happening.

Suddenly she looked at David full in the face, her cheeks streaked with dirt smeared tears, her eyes wide and frightened. "Yes, I do." Then her face went hard and cold. "Do you?" she added.

David suddenly had the feeling he wasn't in control of anything anymore. He felt like he was going to vomit again. He was sure of it. He wanted to move, but his feet held firm. His mind screamed to get away.

"Humanity hasn't changed that much," the woman said to him in an angry hiss. "We still worship the Old Ones. And they still demand their blood. For all we think we've advanced the Old Ones ensure that we know we haven't. May Kuklanoresh save us all, for he is fair and just!" Then her voice got very soft and almost melodic. "This is the work of Siggurath." Then the woman fainted.

David found that he could move again, the urge to vomit was nearly unbearable. Then he saw police officers crowding around the woman.

"What happened here?" a younger officer asked.

"I... I don't know. We were talking and then she just suddenly fainted," David replied.

After the officer dismissed him, David went back to the curb and sat down again. He leaned over and vomited again, and then he started to pray for knowledge and understanding. His mind was still reeling from the strange feeling that had accompanied the old woman's speech. He found it hard to concentrate and focus his mind on God, on Jesus, on the Holy Spirit, the three that he knew beyond a shadow of a doubt would save him. He sighed and bowed his head to pray.

Ben looked around the church but found nothing else that would help him in his examination. He sat down in one of the pews and thought.

He had an unknown person or persons who were involved in an unknown cult. These people go first to the church at the university to kill a priest who is also involved in a cult, or might just be experimenting with circles and Magick on his own. It could also be possible, that the fact that the priest was involved in the Occult has no relevance to the murders at all, and is just excess information. The murderers clean the circle. Why? Unless the fact that the priest is involved in the Occult is an important part of the puzzle. So we bring back the idea that the priest was a planned target and not just some poor soul who was in the wrong place at the wrong time. Then the symbol, what does that mean? It could be the astral symbol for whatever daemon these freaks worship. Then there's the problem of the writing on the wall, that had just occurred to Ben, why go to all the trouble of cleaning the circle and not the wall? That question would not be easily answered.

Now there was the second murder. Ben didn't understand its relevance to the first murder. The victim wasn't a cult member, not that Ben could see anyway. The victim also wasn't a Catholic priest, which doesn't help the theory that was brought to them earlier by the girls and Mike, that it was someone from the cult of Nigorsus. Why kill again? Perhaps the pastor did something that hurt the cult in some way, but what about the tie with the first murder? Nothing, yet. Why change the location of the symbol? Why make it obvious now? Perhaps the first murder was supposed to be a secret, while the second was supposed to be a lesson, but a lesson to whom? People who dare to cross the cult? What cult? What cult is doing this? It's all in the symbol. The answer lies in what the symbol stands for.

Martin walked over to Ben and sat down beside him, flipping up his notebook.

"The night janitor found the body," he said, flipping through his notes. "He came in to investigate a strange noise and saw the pastor on the cross and saw a man in black with a long, black ponytail running out the front door. The pastor was alive when the janitor got there. Died before the first responders could arrive."

Ben looked up and winced at Martin weakly. "Not much to go on."

Martin shook his head and closed his notebook. "No," he replied. "Not much at all. Every investigation starts with nothing, though, so in that respect, we're ahead."

Ben smiled. "I'm going to go check on David."

Martin nodded absently and stared at the body on the cross. "Can we get that poor man off that thing?"

Ben stood and walked outside. He found David sitting on the curb in front of a pool of vomit and staring into the soft snow that had begun to fall.

"David?" Ben said. "You OK?"

David looked up at Ben and filled him in on the encounter with the old lady. By the time he was done, he was weeping openly.

Ben looked away and thought about the cult of Siggurath. "No. It can't be," he said.

"What do you mean?" David asked as he stood up.

"I know what the symbol for Siggurath is, and this isn't it," Ben replied, pulling the sketch David had made from his pocket. "We have to go to an old friend of mine. He'll have the necessary books to help us." Ben turned to go inside. "Wait here, I'll be right back."

Ben walked into the church and found Martin and told him he was going to do some research to find out what the symbol stood for. Then they would be that much closer to finding the people responsible.

"Be careful," Martin said. "You guys are the only Occult experts I have." He smiled as Ben turned to leave.

# Chapter Five

David was confused now. He had clearly received an answer to prayer, maybe not in the most glamorous way but the old woman had answered a prayer by telling him who was responsible for the killings. But Ben told him that it was impossible and that the symbol was not the cult of Siggurath. David found himself doubting what he was certain God had given him.

Father help me, David prayed silently. He bowed his head and waited for an answer, it didn't come. Ben came back out, collected David, and they walked down the street.

"Ben," David said, suddenly, a strange thought coming to his head. "Who's Kuklanoresh?"

Ben looked over to David, surprised. "Where did you hear that name?"

"The lady I told you about mentioned it," David replied. "She said that he would save them all, or something like that."

Ben shook his head. "Kuklanoresh is the true name of a Daemon that has a couple of small cults around here," he explained. "He's in direct opposition to Siggurath for a position at Lucifer's side."

"Why would God give me a message through her then?" David asked.

Ben stopped and faced David. "It might not have been God, David. It could just be Satan trying to confuse us."

David shook his head. "I know it was God," he said, but his voice sounded just a little unsure now.

Four blocks from the church Ben led David to an old run down house. The fence was rotten and falling over, with paint chips which said, at one time, it was white. The windows were all dark and the porch was lopsided and crumbling.

"People live in there?" David asked.

Ben nodded his head. "Yep, this is an old buddy of mine. He's got a library second to none in Canada," he said. "Occultists come from all over the country to use his books."

"Sounds like a nice guy," David said dryly.

Ben looked at David for a moment, then said, "You might just want to go home to the others, David. It's going to be pretty oppressive in there. You seem beat anyway."

"Be careful, Ben. Pray before you go in," David said. "I am beat. Maybe I'll go home and pray with the gang. Don't be long, OK?" David suddenly had a painful pang of guilt in his chest.

Ben nodded and shook David's hand before he walked up to the house. He stood on the front porch and closed his eyes, saying a short prayer for safety before he knocked on the large oak door.

It took David fifteen minutes to get home from the house where he left Ben. He didn't feel comfortable leaving him there alone but David was also having a hard time spiritually understanding what had been revealed to him at the Baptist church, by the old woman. David knew Ben could take care of himself in just about any situation, he had been doing it for a great many years before he met David and he was sure Ben would be fine.

His mind looped over and over between these two thoughts until they became a mixed up jumble of confusion and uncertainty. He tried to separate the two, once, and just couldn't. At one point he thought that Ben was going to talk to the old lady about going to the library.

He took a deep breath and prayed, not really for anything, just prayed, worshiping softly in his mind. He relaxed enough to realize that Ben would be safe. He was going to see an old friend.

Keep telling yourself that, David, he thought with a shake of his head.

When he arrived home, he found that Sara had gone home to study and Marianne and Mike were watching the television.

"Hi, David. Where's Ben?" Marianne asked. She stood and gave David a hug - he nearly broke into tears.

"I... I left him at a house where he was getting some information on the murders."

"Murders?? Plural?" Mike asked.

"There was another one at a Baptist church tonight. We went there and saw it," David began. Then suddenly the entire story came out. The old woman, and what Ben had said, but he said nothing about the uncertainties that he had. He also didn't tell them about the feeling in the pit of his stomach that he had left Ben in danger.

"David, it might be more complex than just one cult angry at God. It's probably much more complex than that," Marianne started. "Trust God, He might have only given you a part of the puzzle. Just the beginning to something that's much more intricate." She sat on the couch and tapped the seat beside her. David sat down and she started to give him a massage to relax his aching muscles. Then the phone rang.

Mike reached over and grabbed it.

"Hello?" he said into the plastic receiver.

"Hi, Mike? It's Sara, are Ben and David back yet?" she said from the other end of the line.

"No, Ben isn't, but David is. Do you want to talk to him?" Mike looked at David as he talked.

"No, I'll be right over. I was praying and I suddenly had a bad feeling. Like something very terrible is going to happen." Then she hung up. Mike laid the phone back in the cradle and looked perplexed for a moment.

"Well, what's up?" Marianne asked.

"That was Sara. She's on her way over. She says she's got a bad feeling about David and or Ben," Mike said.

"No!" David screamed. He sat up and started to put on his coat. "I had the same feeling when I left Ben at that house."

"Wait, David. Ben can take care of himself. Let's just wait, and if it gets too late we'll go and see what's up," Mike said, as he pulled David's coat off.

"I don't like that idea," David muttered stubbornly, but he allowed Mike to put his coat in the closet.

"David, why don't you go upstairs and get some rest," Marianne said.

"No, I'm going to sit up and wait for Ben," David said as he sat in the big plush chair that Ben loved to sit in.

As Ben approached the old house he looked back at David as he walked home. He had the sinking feeling he would never see his friend again and had to overcome the urge to run to the slowly walking man. Ben turned his attention to the door and knocked heavily on it. A moment later it opened to reveal a tall thin man with long black hair. He was dressed head to toe in black and his piercing eyes were lined with thick black liner. He smiled softly when he saw Ben standing there.

"Gideon, how pleasant to see you again," the man spoke with a soft British accent. Ben knew it was merely a fabrication that was designed to make him seem more regal.

"Raven," Ben nodded. "It's been a while, old friend." Ben could play the stoic game too.

Raven moved aside to allow Ben in. As the door closed behind him Ben found it sounded a great deal like a coffin lid closing. Calm down, Ben. You're going to screw up if you let your mind wander, Ben thought. He looked around and saw the various implements of magick. Candles lit the room and incense burned in the daemon shaped holder on the coffee table.

Just as I remember it, Ben thought. "You haven't changed the place much," he said out loud.

"Change disrupts the way we conduct our energy. You know that, Gideon," Raven smiled.

"I haven't heard that name in awhile. It seems like a different person now," Ben replied, as he sat on the couch.

"Maybe it is." Raven sat in a chair across from Ben and smiled again. "Tea?" he offered.

He knows that to refuse him I would be being rude and he won't help me. But I've got a real bad feeling about this, Ben thought.

"Yes, please," Ben said softly. As Raven poured some tea out of a pot into black teacups, Ben stood and looked at a painting of a red dragon on the wall. "I need the use of your library for a few hours."

Raven handed a cup to Ben, who thanked him but didn't drink.

"Why?" he asked.

"I'm looking for a specific symbol of a specific cult." Ben turned to face his host.

"Again I ask why?" Raven watched Ben with intense interest.

"If it was important for you to know I would tell you. But it isn't," Ben parried.

"I don't want any unwanted interest in my sect, or myself, Gideon," Raven replied.

Ben thought for a moment. He could tell him why, what would it hurt. "I'm working on the murder of the priest at Assumption. We found a symbol and I want to know what cult it is," he said, watching Raven's expressions.

Raven's face didn't move. "How did you get to be working on that murder?"

Ben smiled and sipped lightly at the tea. "That is of no interest to you." Ben knew that how he got involved couldn't hurt Raven or his sect in any way.

Raven turned and walked back to his chair, then turned with a sly smile and said, "There now, that didn't hurt at all now did it. You know where the library is." Raven turned and sat in the chair again.

Ben walked downstairs to the library, the room was small and dusty and the walls were lined floor to ceiling with books. Most of them were old and worn, but some were new and had only recently been read. Ben scanned the titles of the books until he found the one he wanted, The Necronomicon. Raven was one of three people in the world who had a completely translated version of the book in English. The book was deemed to be too dangerous; the publishers translated it in three different languages. In order to get the entire book one had to find the three different copies and have the other two translated into English. It took a long time but it could be done. As Raven proved.

Ben said a short prayer for protection against daemons before he opened the book. He scanned its pages until he found the spot he wanted. He looked over each symbol, comparing them to David's sketch until he found the match. The cult of Ctchutic. Ben looked up from the book and a shock of fear went through his body. That was Raven's cult. Ben remembered Raven talking about it shortly before he was saved. Raven was moving to a more organized cult, and Ben was starting to draw away from the occult.

A man in black with a black ponytail! That was what Martin said the description of the murderer was. He slammed the book shut and stood up suddenly frightened. As he turned to leave the library his head exploded in a flash of light and pain. Then everything went dark.

It was cold. That was the first thing Ben noticed when he woke up.

His hands were tied behind his back in loose knots and a gag was jammed half heartedly into his mouth. After a moment of fidgeting he. managed to loosen the knots so he could pull his hands free of the rope.

As he stood he pulled the gag out of his mouth and threw it onto the ground. After a quick look about the room he decided he was in the old coal bin in Raven's basement. The door was made of a shabbily constructed wood and Ben laughed at it thinking, Raven knows I was trained in martial arts, I wonder why he put me here?

Ben whipped his leg around and brought it up hard against the door, smashing it to splinters. He quickly ran out into the dark hall beyond. Suddenly he heard banging and shuffling overhead.

"Footsteps," Ben whispered to himself. "I've got to learn to be quieter." He darted up the hall, and to the door at the end, bursting into the room.

The room was darkened and lit by only a few burning candles along the black walls. There was a large circle painted on the floor, in paint as dark as coal and dried blood stains littered the centre of the circle. At the front of the room, the most prominent thing, was a large stone alter cut from granite.

As Ben quickly surveyed the room, he noticed a window, slightly ajar at the front of the room, behind the altar.

"I thank you, Jesus, for an exit, but couldn't you have put it somewhere else?" Ben said dryly.

As Ben moved toward the window the door burst open again and a rough voice called,

"Stop, you!"

"Yeah, right!" Ben said as he broke into a run and leapt at the window. "Like that's number one on my list of things to do."

Now would be a really good time to take all us Christians home, God, Ben thought.

As he pulled himself out of the basement, Ben felt a hand grab his leg, a quick jerk of it sent the unknown assailant into the altar, knocking it over and sent the attacker sprawling onto the floor.

For the first time, Ben noticed he didn't have his jacket. The cold snow and wind bit into his body mercilessly as he pulled himself to a standing position. His head suddenly swam with dizziness and throbbed where he had been struck. Taking a few steps Ben found that he had to rest against a tree for support.

The front door flew open and someone ran out of the house waving a metal object in Ben's direction. A flash lit the night sky for a brief second followed by a sudden crack of what sounded like thunder and splinters of wood flew into Ben's face, scratching and cutting him .

Bringing up all the energy he could, Ben pushed his.body into a steady run away from the house. Another shot rang out in the silence of the night. A burning pain ripped through Ben's side and he fell hard into a snow bank, staining the white snow red with his blood.

"Stop!" Ben heard. "No shooting! Let him go, we can't afford to cause any commotion now." It didn't sound like Raven's voice. It did sound very familiar though, but Ben couldn't place it.

Ben glanced back and saw Raven standing on the front porch with another man dressed in black beside him, Ben couldn't see the other man's face, but as he turned he saw the long, black ponytail swish behind him, leaving Raven on the porch alone.

Ben stood again and stumbled up the street. The snow was starting to fly freely swirling in mini snow hurricanes, stinging his face and causing his eyes to water. Ben knew it was another fifteen minutes walk to his home, but he was sure that he wouldn't make it. Not, wet, cold and bleeding.

His mind began to create pictures that seemed to fly with the snow. Pretty pictures of fairies and sprites dancing on glassy floors of ice. Little flashes of light that moved swiftly and gracefully as the snow fell all around, creating a gentle blanket that covered the earth. He tried to focus on putting one foot in front of the other. He could feel the blood running down his side, it seemed cold to him, everything was cold now.

Ben stumbled and fell, his body wet with sweat and melted snow, his hair falling in gentle curls around his closing eyes. He rolled painfully onto his back, his hand trying to keep his precious blood in his body. He absently wondered why he was sweating, because he felt so cold.

"God," Ben said softly, the words tasting like iron in his mouth. "God, Father, I need you now. I need you, Jesus. Please send someone, send someone for me, Jesus. If it's your will, I'll die here, Lord. But please, if my work isn't finished, send someone." The last few words slurred out of his mouth like water falling over rocks. And just as Ben's eyes closed he saw a white light fall over him and a darkened silhouette reach down to his head.

David sat in the chair waiting for the phone to ring. Ben had been gone for six hours now, at the second hour Sara arrived from her house to keep vigil as they waited for Ben to return. At the third hour, Sara and Marianne fell asleep on the couch. At the fourth hour David had called Martin, who promised to go out and search for Ben himself. At the fifth hour the blizzard started. And now, at the sixth hour, David sat up and waited for Ben to return. He was the only one left awake. Mike went to sleep fifteen minutes ago and now David sat alone in the house.

Alone, waiting for news, he prayed.

Then there was a sharp rap on the front door, David leapt from his chair-to answer it. As he pulled the big oak door open he was met with Martin's broad features. The first thing David noticed was that the big police officer was alone. His hopes suddenly fell.

"You ... you couldn't find him?" David whispered softly, so that he wouldn't wake the girls sleeping on the couch.

Martin shook his head. "No. I searched most of the west end of the city and he was nowhere to be found." The words seemed like a death sentence to David's ears. "I checked the area around the address you gave me but there was nothing there. I'd like to report him as missing, but he has to be gone for up to twenty-four hours," he added.

David turned and walked back into the house, his last hope was gone, Martin hadn't found him. In his heart he knew that Ben was in trouble. He knew something was wrong with his friend. He knew it!

But he was helpless to do anything for him.

He had been praying all evening, but it felt like his prayers were hitting the roof of the house and just bouncing back at him in a mockery of what he believed. They seemed to say to him, there is no use praying, no one is listening to you.

Martin closed the door and sat in a wooden rocker that rested by the dying embers of the fire David made a few hours earlier.

"Don't worry, David. He's probably just talking with his friend," Martin said softly.

David looked up and Martin was surprised with the haunted expression on his face. "No," he said. "Something is very wrong."

Gentle hands lifted Ben's body up, cradling him against warm flesh. Ben's eyes refused to focus on the face of the man, or was it a woman? The features wouldn't come clear in his mind. He felt the sensation of being moved as if he was on a ship, the gentle swaying back and forth rocking him to sleep.

"Who ... ?" Ben tried to speak, but the words were caught in his throat, and the strength didn't exist to push them clear.

"S-h-h-h," a soft melodic voice said. It was definitely a man. A man with the most beautiful voice Ben had ever heard. A voice of a thousand clear bells ringing in his mind. "Rest now, you are safe."

Ben tried to speak again and found that he couldn't. The gentle swaying of the man's even walk was slowly rocking him to sleep. Ben couldn't help but be relaxed by the stranger's soft voice as he gently hummed a tune Ben was certain he had heard before. Ben's head turned back and his eyes focused on the spot where he had, only moments before, been lying in the snow, dying.

The last thing Ben remembered before he fell asleep, was that there were no footprints in the snow.

The soft knocking on the door was what woke David up. Martin was already on his feet and moving toward it. Marianne and Sara were up and standing by the window trying to see if it was Ben at the door, after a moment, David heard Sara gasp. David stood and followed

Martin as he pulled the door open to reveal a gentle looking man carrying a second man. David immediately recognized the man in the stranger's arms as Ben.

The stranger walked into the house and put Ben on the couch. David immediately noticed the dark red patch of blood on Ben's side and went wordlessly to the phone to call an ambulance.

"Ben!" Sara was crying into his bloodstained shirt. Tears streaked her soft face and she gently wiped Ben's sweat-soaked hair out of his closed eyes.

Then the stranger laid a fine-boned hand on Sara's shoulder and crouched beside the weeping girl. His downy, blond hair fell about his slim shoulders as he quietly said, "He will live."

Sara looked up into the stranger's eyes. Suddenly all fear left her, she found herself lost in the deep, blue orbs. She saw gentleness, assurance, and strength she had never seen before in any human being. Then, suddenly, the stranger stood and the moment was broken,

Marianne and Martin stood beside each other in confusion as the man turned to the door. There was a brief moment when his eyes locked on the two that stood silently behind Sara, who turned back to Ben and was stroking his hair away from his face. The stranger stopped at the door, turned to David and locked eyes with him for a moment, David set the phone down without dialing any numbers.

"He heard," the man said. Then he turned and left the house. David suddenly ran to the door. Who was this stranger that came into his house with his friend, beaten and bleeding? What was his name? Where did he come from? Where did he find Ben? How did he know to bring him here? There were so many unanswered questions. He wanted to know. And that last statement, it was made directly to him. Why did he said that? How had he known?

He arrived at the door and ripped it open.

"Who are ... ?" David started.

The street was empty. David walked out onto the front porch, his mind suddenly reeling with ideas. Behind him, in the house, he heard Martin talking about needing to catalogue Ben's wounds. He stared out at the falling snow for the mysterious man. He was nowhere to be found. David examined the blanket of snow which covered the ground. No footprints lead away from the house. None but David's even left the door.

Martin ran out to the door and grabbed David by the shoulder, spinning him around and smiling broadly at him.

"He's fine, David," Martin said with a grin. "There's no injury, the blood must be someone else's."

David turned and saw that Ben was sleeping soundly on the couch.

His chest was rising and falling steadily and peacefully. His face looked quiet and serene.

Sara stood, said she was tired and was going home to get some sleep. She had been very calm, David noticed, since the stranger spoke those words to her. "He will live," that was all he said. Those words calmed her down to the point where she felt she could go home to get some much needed sleep.

David wondered where this mysterious man came from. He knew nothing about him. What he could figure out from his observations? The man was obviously strong and kind, Ben weighed at least 200lbs. Who else would have carried Ben back to the house? Unless of course Ben knew the man. But David was sure he knew most of the people Ben knew. Who was this stranger who brought Ben back to them, and then disappeared like a shadow in the night?

No footprints. The stranger left no footprints, even on the porch where he must have stepped to leave the house. That's what bothered David the most about the entire episode. The man left no footprints.

Unless, of course, he wasn't a man.

# Chapter Six

Ben woke the following morning, lying in his bed at the old Victorian house on California street. His head throbbed with a dull ache which, he assumed, was the result of the hit in the back of the head he took the night before. He remembered little of what happened after the man picked him up, except he had felt safe. His eyes focused, somewhat, on the wall that stood opposite his bed. There was a vague human shape there and he couldn't quite make out who it was, although it was a familiar shape.

"Who is it?" Ben said weakly.

"Raven, my friend." Ben started back in shock. What was he doing here? "There is no need to be afraid. I'm not here to hurt you," Raven assured him. "I'm here as your friend."

Ben slowly eased himself up on the bed until he reached a rough sitting position. His eyes were slowly beginning to focus on Raven's delicate elf-like features.

"What do you want?" Ben asked, guardedly.

"I wanted to tell you I had nothing to do with the murders," Raven replied.

"Then who does? We found the Ctchutic symbol at the murders, Raven," Ben spat out. "That's your cult!"

Raven sat in a chair at the foot of the bed. "You have a nice room," he said. "I am afraid, however, I had to sneak in the window. A skill you taught me which has proved to be invaluable." Then he tossed an old book onto Ben's lap.

Ben looked down at the book and was shocked to see an old copy of the Bible sitting on his legs. Raven must have found out Ben collected old Bibles.

"My sources tell me it was carried at one time by Alexander Brock," Raven said with a smile.

"Why?" he asked, his face skeptical of the unexpected gift.

"I felt I owed you something for the rude way some of my followers treated you," Raven said as he smoothed out the wrinkles in the blankets on Ben's legs.

"I assumed it was something you ordered .... " Ben couldn't find the words to say what he was thinking.

"No," Raven said as he locked eyes with Ben. "I am and always will be your friend."

Ben studied Raven for a long time before he spoke. "I said that to you," he said. Then he paused, "A long time ago."

"Not so long in my mind," Raven said. Then he stood and pulled on his long, black trench coat. "I must go."

"Wait," Ben said suddenly, not knowing why he stopped Raven from leaving. His clouded mind reeled for an excuse to keep his old friend in the room. "You never told me who was involved in the murders."

Raven stopped and looked intently at Ben for a moment. "Will you join me again, Gideon?" he said as he turned to approach Ben's bed. "Will you explore the boundaries of the living and the dead with me one more time?"

Ben was startled with the sudden plea from Raven and he stared at Raven in silence for a moment before responding. "I can't, Raven. I did it once and that was enough for me," he said. "I don't want to anymore."

Raven straightened his coat and walked to the window, then he turned again to Ben. He looked like he wanted to say something but then lowered his head.

"Raven!" Ben called before the black clad man could open the window. "Who was the other man with you on the porch?"

"My sect has nothing to do with the murders," Raven said without raising his head. Then he opened the window and leapt out into the darkness, his trench coat opening like wings.

Ben laid back in his bed and thought about his unexpected visit. It seemed like he had gotten no information from Raven but as he mulled over the conversation he found that there was much more in what Raven said than just the fact that he wanted Ben to join him again.

He had said that his sect wasn't involved in the murders.

That was important because Raven's sect was only those people in Windsor. It didn't include the people outside of Windsor. Ben laid back and smiled, thanking Jesus that Raven felt it in his heart to give Ben that much information at least.

"Ben," Marianne said that morning at breakfast. "You are perhaps the most blessed person I have ever met in my life."

Ben smiled at his blond haired friend. "Well, one has one's crosses to bear," he replied with a smile.

"Hello!" came the familiar voice of Martin from the front door.

"Come on in, Martin!" David called.

"How are you guys doing?" Martin asked as he sat at the kitchen table.

"We were just saying how blessed Ben is," Michael supplied.

"Yeah, he sure is one lucky guy," Martin said.

"Luck has nothing to do with it," Sara said. "Ben has a gift from God. Jesus has been watching out for him for a long time now. This shooting is just one example of that."

"Well, I've been with the force a long time and I've never seen anyone quite so ... blessed as him," Martin laughed. "By the way, if you guys are such good Christians, then why do you know so much about the Occult?"

"Ben was involved with it before he came to Jesus," Marianne said. Then she noticed Ben's haunted expression at the mention of his past. "He doesn't like to talk about it much," she added.

Mike came over with a pile of pancakes on a large platter and an extra plate for Martin. They ate breakfast in silence and no one even attempted conversation, the breakfast was so good. After they had finished eating, David and Sara went to do the dishes while Martin leaned back and took a long drink of his coffee.

"An excellent breakfast, Mike," he exclaimed.

"Thank you," Mike said with a mock bow.

"Tell us, Martin," Ben said. "Are you married?"

Martin looked surprised at the sudden question and was silent for a moment. "I was, once," he said quietly. "A long time ago."

Ben felt ashamed for bringing such a painful topic up. "I'm sorry, I didn't...."

"Hey!" Martin interrupted. "It's OK. If you guys and me are going to work together for a little while then you should know a little about me."

"Still..." Ben started.

"It's OK," Martin said, forcing a smile. "Look, I've got to go to work right now. I just wanted to drop by and make sure you guys were OK. Also, the pastor that was killed the other night. His name was Owen Reynolds, he was apparently very outspoken against the Occult. Maybe you guys can dig something up at the library again, since that Nigorsus thing fell through." Martin stood and walked to the door and turned. "Hey, guys. We'll get them," Martin smiled, and then left.

That afternoon the small group decided to go to the library again and see what they could dig up on the Occult, specifically in Windsor. Marianne, David and Mike went to the library, while Sara insisted on staying behind to take care of Ben. Ben just planned to sleep anyway, she could get some studying done.

When they arrived at the library they each took a large bound tome that held months worth of Windsor's newspapers inside and sat down to begin their research for anything that would connect pastor Reynolds criticisms and the Occult.

For hours they searched the large books until David slammed his book shut, removed his glasses and rubbed his tired eyes.

"I think I'm going cross-eyed," he mumbled.

Mike closed his book and went off to get another one. As he passed David, he clapped him on the shoulder. "Hold on, David," he said. "This is where most of the work gets done, I expect." David rolled his eyes.

Marianne closed her book and sat across from him, taking David's hand in hers.

"I know it seems impossible, doesn't it?" she asked.

"No, it's not that. It's just that there's so much to look at," David replied. "I'm having a hard time remembering what we're looking for," he laughed softly.

"Well, if you can laugh it can't be all that bad," Mike said as he returned with another book.

"Mike," David said with a smile. "Has anyone ever told you you're too positive?"

Mike sat down and chuckled softly to himself.

David sat in silence as Marianne and Mike went back to looking at the headlines. He had been thinking again and again about what Ben had said. It couldn't be the Siggurath cult. The symbols are wrong, Ben even found out the symbol was for the Cult of Ctchutic. But he was certain the information was given by God, through the old woman.

David was getting confused now, and to top it all off he was having problems sleeping and he couldn't pray with the same vigor and joy he once had. He was afraid to tell the others because of what he thought they would say to him. He was the one that brought the cult problem to them, and now he was the one that couldn't stand to work it out. To David that was as bad as giving up on what God had ordered him to do in the Bible. Battle Satan wherever you find him. Even if it had to mean losing a little sleep over it.

"I've got it!" Mike whispered. David stood and wearily trudged over to the large man. Marianne peered over Mike's other shoulder as he spoke.

"Here," He pointed to an article that's headline ran: "Local Clergy Engages in Debate With Cult Leaders" He turned to face the others, "What it says is that a bunch of clergy got together and had it out with a bunch of cultists. The clergy included the priest that was killed on the first night and the pastor that was killed the other night.

"Here's the neat part though, the cultists included a guy from T.O. named Robert Darkfall, He's the Ontario leader for the cult of Ctchutic. Also there is another guy named Joshua Smith, he's the High Priest of the cult of Siggurath. They were the leaders of the cultists side of the debate."

Marianne had been reading over Mike's shoulder and then said, "It says here that because of the social and political stigmas that have been put on cult activity the entire debate was a loss for the cultists. Praise God!"

"Let's get a copy of this and bring it home," David said. "Martin's going to want to see this." David was sure Joshua Smith must be involved somehow. The leader of the Cult of Siggurath. That made David's belief in the information all the stronger. He left the library with more confidence and hope than he had arrived with.

Raven was thinking. He had done some research into Ben and his friends. But he still had a lot of unanswered questions. Why was Ben involved in this investigation? How was Raven's sect going to deal with the sudden interest? He decided the only way he was going to get any real answers was to call his Superior.

Raven lifted the phone and dialed the number. "Good evening," came the deep voiced response to the ringing.

"Good evening, Superior," Raven said.

"Good evening, Raven. What can I do for you?" the deep voiced man asked.

"I am calling regarding the unfortunate circumstances surrounding Gideon's visit the other night, Robert," Raven said.

"What about it?" Robert replied coldly.

"It is causing me some difficulties."

"What kind of difficulties?"

"A small band of university students has taken it upon themselves to assist a Police detective in the investigation."

"What does this have to do with Gideon's visit the other night?" Robert paused for a moment and then said, "Tell me, who are the others?"

"There is David Masterson, Sara Blanchard, Marianne Storm and Mike McIssic; they are the university students. The detective is Greg Martin," Raven replied.

"We will have to do something to lead them off our scent then won't we? I'll call you back in a few minutes," Robert said and he hung up the phone.

Raven replaced the receiver in the cradle and walked to where a wall was covered in framed pictures. He reached up and pulled one down from its place in the collage.

The picture portrayed two young men, perhaps seventeen or eighteen, soaking wet and standing in front of a waterfall. The taller man had long, straight, lustrous black hair and the shorter had even longer, curly, brown hair. The brown haired man looked up at the taller one and smiled, while the black haired man grinned at the camera.

"What happened to us, Gideon?" Raven asked the shorter man.

"Do you remember this time? Do you remember what you said?"

"Guys, go stand in front of the waterfall," Kristan had called to Raven and Gideon. Kristan was a streamlined young man of seventeen with a short, neat cut and a struggling mustache which he adored.

"I've got to pull the canoe up out of the water," Gideon replied.

"Get over here," Raven said. "It'll only take a minute."

Gideon left the canoe and walked over to the spot where Kristan was pointing. He turned and scowled into the camera.

"At least look like you know the guy, Gideon," Kristan said.

"How's this?" Gideon said as he looped an arm under Raven's and flipped him in to the water behind them. Gideon stepped back, slipped and fell on top of his waterlogged friend. Kristan stood on the bank laughing in glee.

"Get out of there, you two," he howled.

Gideon helped Raven to his feet and the two of them pulled themselves out of the water.

"Raven, you know something?" Gideon asked.

"I know a lot of things. What?" Raven replied.

"I am now, and always will be your friend," Gideon said up to the tall man beside him.

"Smile!" said Kristan the camera click-whirred, and the moment was preserved forever in time.

"Then the boat floated away and we had to chase it up the river," Raven smiled at the picture.

The phone rang, startling Raven, who dropped the picture. The glass shattered and Raven turned to answer the phone, stopping for only a moment to look back at the shattered glass.

"Good evening," Raven said as he stared at the broken glass on the floor.

"Good evening, Raven," Robert's voice said back to him.

"How may I help, Robert?" Raven said as he pulled his eyes away from the glass that seemed to taunt him.

"I just got off the phone with the Concierge of the Siggurath cult. His name is Joshua Smith," Robert said.

Raven thought for a moment. "What does he have to do with our problem?"

"You need not worry about that," Robert said. "He, however has an excellent idea how to lead those students off our backs. See that they find their way to Toronto. Smith owes a favour to a man in Timmins, Ontario and one of those girls will do just fine."

"They already know the cult is involved in the murders. I expect that they will follow the chain up and come to you anyway," Raven replied.

"Ensure they do," Robert said. "The Siggurath cult is powerful and I want to make her a present to Smith. Then he will give her to the man in Timmins and they will be out of our hair. They won't dare continue once one of their girls is missing." Then he hung up the phone.

Raven returned to the shattered picture frame and stood over it for a moment.

"What happened to us, Gideon?" he said again. "Where has our friendship gone? What have we become?" As he stared down at the picture through the shattered glass he noticed a small drop of water on it, then another. He reached up and touched his eye, it was wet with tears.

"What have I become?"

Brad Montgomery was a small, thin man, with small, thin dreams. He was a poor cop that was promoted more because it was less dangerous to have him in administration then on the street. With the contacts that he made within the cult that his wife had introduced to him, he quickly became the Chief of Police.

Now he was a small, thin man sitting behind a large desk and ignoring the large, thick muscled detective that stood in front of him.

Martin stood and waited. The office was small and held a number of important awards and certificates and medals. The sketchbook for a successful career. He stood before the desk with the thin, white shirted man ignoring him for the better part of five minutes. Finally Brad Montgomery looked up.

"I want the clergy murders case finished quick," he said.

Martin replied, "Sir we're tracking down the man responsible."

The man in the white shirt shook his head. "What you've got is a whole bunch of Occult garbage. What I want is a person in my holding cell being charged with two counts first degree murder."

“Well my ‘Occult garbage’ experts just got me a couple of names,” Martin replied. “I’m going to need to go to Toronto for a few days to interview them.”

Montgomery glared for a moment, then turned back to his desk. “You have enough of a backlog, I’ll send Johnstone to accompany your experts.”

Martin shook his head, “There’s no real need to send them to Toronto for this. They’re all students and I don’t want them to suffer in their studies.” Martin was a little confused about why he suddenly felt so strongly about the students going to Toronto without him.

“They’ve been on the cutting edge of this case from the start,” Montgomery smiled. “Why stop now?”

Martin turned and slowly moved out of the office, his mind unable to take in the fact that he had just lost the case to Johnstone, a young detective that was rumoured to go to the same church as Montgomery. He stepped out of the police station and toward his car, where a man in a dark suit stood in the slush beside his car door.

"Detective Martin?" the man asked.

"Yes?" Martin asked.

"I have a special order for you," the man said. "I know your chief has taken you off the Clergy Murders case."

Martin nodded. "Yeah so?"

"I have a court order here that gives you full powers to follow this case as far as you can," the man said, as he held up a piece of paper. "I'll hold on to this for the time being. If you need it I'll be there." The man turned and started to leave.

"What about my Chief?" Martin asked.

"My boss outranks your boss," the man said as he walked away. Martin smiled and got into his car.

From a window high above the parking lot, Brad Montgomery let the curtain fall and lifted his iPhone.

"Robert?" he said. "There may be a small problem with Martin. The Pentecostals are involved now."

The next day Martin came in excited and eagerly asking for everyone to get together that night. Ben asked what all the fuss was about, but Martin refused to give any information until the girls arrived.

When they did, Martin sat dramatically in the high-backed chair by the fireplace and slowly settled himself in. The room got very quiet in anticipation of his announcement; Martin noticed the fire in the fireplace was dying. He calmly got up and prodded at it with the poker until it built itself back up to a warming blaze.

"Martin, would you just get to the point!" Ben said eagerly.

"OK, Ben, relax," Martin leaned back in his chair and got comfortable.

"Martin," David said impatiently.

"Now," Martin began. "I had a meeting today with a guy that's keeping me on the Clergy murders case. He said I have permission to go to Toronto to follow up on the leads you guys brought to me regarding the connection with the debate and the murders. My chief managed to get in there that I had to bring my 'Occult experts' with me."

"We really aren't experts," Mike said.

"Compared to most of the police force you are," Martin replied. “That struck me as odd, but it will be good to have you guys here that understand this stuff more than I do.

"Anyway, I have permission to take my Occult experts to Toronto for the weekend to follow up on the murders." Martin smiled. "In other words, we're going to nail those jerks to the wall. And you guys can come with me if you want."

The small group looked around at each other in amazement. Doubt, joy and fear were mixed in their faces and no one spoke until Marianne stood up.

"I think we should go," Marianne said. "We've been attacked spiritually, and Ben's even been shot at because of these guys. But those things aren't the reasons why we should go. We should go to battle Satan. We should go to do God's work and to make sure this doesn't continue. We should go to end the reign that this cult has had on our lives, in the name of Jesus Christ!"

Marianne looked around and one by one each person in turn nodded their head adding their own "Praise God!"'s, or "Yes!"'s.

Martin stood and said, "We leave tomorrow morning at seven o'clock. Meet me at the train station at six-thirty." Then Martin stood and went to the door. "This means much to you, I know. Don't worry, we'll get them." Then he left.

Ben stood and went upstairs to start packing. Mike quickly fol- lowed and David offered to drive the girls to their house to get their things ready.

"Can we stay here tonight?" Marianne asked. "It will be easier to leave tomorrow if we're all at the same place."

"Yes," David said. He quietly got his coat on and went outside to start his car.

Marianne got into the front seat of David's car, and Sara crawled into the back. The ride to the girl's house was a quiet one. The tension on David only increased by the fact that Marianne was so close to him.

They arrived at the house and David waited in the car while Marianne and Sara packed their things.

The drive home was just as quiet as the drive to the girls house had been. David stayed very distant despite the attempts of Marianne to get him to talk. When Marianne tried to get David to talk he would merely shrug off any comments or questions with half thought out answers.

When they arrived at the guys house, David quickly helped get the girls set in for the night in the spare room and then he went to bed himself.

# Chapter Seven

They met Martin at the train station at six-thirty the next morning. When they arrived, Martin handed out their tickets and apologized for the fact they were only coach.

"It's the city, you know. We're on a tight budget, or so they say," he said with a smile.

"Well, I've got some news that will make the city happy," Marianne said. "I called up an old friend of ours in Toronto. Collette Pearson, she and her husband say we can stay with them while we're there."

"Hey, that's great news!" Martin exclaimed. "No scummy second rate hotel!"

Marianne looked over at Mike almost apologetically. "She says Christine is visiting with them too."

Mike's face became haunted for a moment, then he wordlessly picked up his bags and walked toward the train.

"What's wrong with him?" Martin asked.

"He and Christine were going out for a while last year," Sara explained. "It was quite serious. They were even talking about getting married."

"What happened?" Martin asked as he followed Sara to the waiting train.

"Well, Christine moved to London to go to Western University."

Sara looked up at the big man. "Mike couldn't stand being away from her, so he broke up with her. He figured it wouldn't hurt as much."

"That's ridiculous!" Martin exclaimed.

"Yes, it is," Sara said. "That's the sad part, they both know it, but they both think the other is happy with the situation so they don't say anything."

They boarded the train and took their seats. Mike sat with Martin, Marianne sat with David, and Sara sat with Ben.

Mike sat in silence for the beginning of the trip, looking out the window at the white blanketed landscape that flew by. Martin sat beside him wondering if he should mention the subject of Christine to him. He still wasn't sure of his relationship with the young man because it was still so new. He wrestled with the problem for most of the trip until he decided to speak.

"Mike, tell me about Christine," he said softly.

"Not much to tell. We went out for awhile and it didn't work out," Mike replied, not looking away from the window.

"Why did you break up?" Martin asked.

"She was moving away and I don't feel that long distant relationships work. It was a good decision for both of us," Mike said, he continued to stare out the window and Martin noticed the slight flutter in his voice.

"If it was, then why are you wishing you hadn't come with us?" Mike turned angrily and glared at the big detective for a moment before silently looking back out the window. "It was," he said softly.

"Do you wish you still had the relationship with her?" Martin asked.

Mike stared out the window, wishing he could become a part of the landscape, free and unhindered. "I do," he whispered.

"Do you still love her?" Martin pressed softly.

Martin could see Mike's reflection in the window and saw the tears that were running down his face.

"Yes," Mike replied. "I do."

Martin put a big hand on Mike's shoulder and said softly, "Then tell her, son. Tell her."

Mike stared out the window, tears dripping onto his coat lapels now and didn't see the landscape anymore. All he saw was the face of Christine reflected back to him.

David sat in silence beside Marianne. His mind raced about the possibilities of what could be interfering, and making it difficult for him to pray. He was becoming more and more distant to his friends, and he knew it. He was having more and more personal problems, yet he didn't know how to cope with them. He felt he couldn't trust anyone, including God.

Marianne sat beside David tom between whether or not she should bring up the subject of David's odd behaviour. What if he got angry. She couldn't see David getting angry, but the way he'd been acting lately ... she didn't know.

Marianne looked at David and for a moment caught his eyes.

David's eyes immediately softened and his hand reached tentatively up to almost touch Marianne's cheek. As she looked down at David's strong hands she was amazed to find that he was shaking; like a child alone in a dark room. David's eyes were locked onto Marianne's. He peered deep into her soft blue eyes and was sure he saw the answers to all of his problems, locked deep inside her mind, just out of reach.

"I..." David started softly. Then he found he couldn't speak any longer, he was lost in those, pale, blue eyes.

Marianne reached down, and touched David's hand, bringing it closer to her face. As soon as he brushed her cheek, he pulled back sharply and turned to face the aisle.

Marianne started back, shocked at the suddenness of his movement and touched his shoulder. "David ... I didn't ... " she started.

"No. Please," David whispered as he shrugged her hand off his shoulder.

They arrived at Union station at two o'clock in the afternoon. There they saw the smiling face of Collette Pearson peering at them through the crowd. As soon as she caught sight of the University group, she raced toward them at full speed until her chubby, dark skinned face was smiling in front of them. Collette gave each person a warm hug and when she got to Martin she stopped and extended her hand.

"Hi, I'm Collette," she said warmly.

"Hello, I'm Detective Greg Martin. Everyone just calls me Martin," the big man replied as he accepted the outstretched hand.

"Good, now that I know you ... " Collette leapt forward and gave the surprised detective a big hug.

"I'll help with the bags." Jeff, Collette's husband, was approaching, and waving to the small group in the train terminal.

Immediately behind Jeff, a girl with long brown hair followed. She approached nervously and gave happy hugs to everyone, but stopped when she reached Mike.

"Hello, Mike. You're looking good," she said softly.

Mike looked up from the floor and looked into her dark green eyes.

"Hello, Christine. You look good too," he replied, then he picked up his bags and followed the rest of the group to the waiting van that would take them to Collette and Jeff's house.

When they arrived at Collette's house, they were amazed at the size of it. The modern brick house would easily have room for the group from Windsor, plus three or four more people. Collette showed them to their rooms, and then said she would have dinner ready in a couple of hours. Martin asked if she had a room where they could sit and talk for a little while. Collette showed them to the library.

The library was a large room with floor to ceiling bookshelves, overflowing with books, on all four walls. Martin took a seat on an old, rocking chair, which had to its personality, a comfortable creak.

"Alright, we have to decide what we're going to do tomorrow. Any ideas?" Martin said in a businesslike manner.

"Well, you're the detective. What do you think we should do?" Ben asked.

"OK, here's what I think," Martin started with a grin. “David, Ben and I will go and see this Robert Darkfall guy. He's the leader of the cult that belongs to the symbol we found in the churches. We'll ask him a few questions, just to see what happens. Mike, you and the girls will go to the library, newspaper, city hall or whatever, and find out as much as you can about this guy. How's that sound for a plan?" Martin smiled.

The small group looked about at each other and smiled.

"Sounds good, Martin," Sara said. “Not that any of us have any expertise to actually argue with you about it.”

That evening after dinner, the group and their hosts sat in the large living room. They sat and talked. Collette, Jeff and Christine were filled in on the accounts of the previous few days, and they filled the small band of cult chasers in on what things had been happening in their lives.

Mike and Christine sat together on the couch. After a short while they talked privately in hushed tones. Once in a while they smiled and reached tentatively out to touch the other, but the hand was always brought back sharply.

They talked until late in the night and then the small group decided they should get some sleep for the busy day before them. So they said their good-nights and went into their rooms. Sleep came slowly for David, and when it did come, it was more of a nightmare and gave him no rest, just haunted his dreams and was now slowly working its way into his waking hours too.

He awoke from his sleep, covered in sweat and shook off the warm covers. Putting his feet on the thick, plush carpet, he walked downstairs to the kitchen to make himself some tea.

He filled the kettle and put it on the stove, then sat down on a chair and rubbed his tired eyes.

It was the kitchen door that startled him. It opened and Christine walked through with a tired face. David smiled up at her and said:

"You startled me. What are you doing up so late?" He pushed a chair out for her to sit in, and as she sat she said:

"I just couldn't sleep. It's the Mike thing."

"Want some tea?" David stood as the kettle began to whistle.

Christine nodded and he poured two cups in silence. When he sat down again, Christine said:

"I don't know what to do. He's not even accepting the fact that he still has feelings for me."

David sipped his tea. "I don't know what to say. 1 mean it's no big secret that he still loves you, but we have to wait until the Lord tells him it's OK to be with you again."

"I don't think 1 can wait that long," Christine said defeated.

"Don't say that. Just spend time in the Word and be with God. It will happen, you just got to have faith," David replied.

Christine looked up and smiled. "I've got that."

David smiled back a small voice in the back of his head said to take his own advice; he asked Christine how school was going for her, rather than acknowledge the voice. They sat and talked for a long time and drank four cups each before they went back to bed. David looked at his bed and sighed. He looked over at Ben, who was sleeping in the bed beside him. How he wished he could sleep peacefully. He prayed for them to stop, the horrible dreams, but they wouldn't, he prayed for strength but it didn't seem to come. What could he do?

David climbed back into his bed, and pulled the covers up around him. He eventually fell asleep. But he never rested.

# Chapter Eight

The morning came far too soon for David. He sat groggily at the breakfast table and ate his toast. Then he slowly and tiredly went to the living room to meet with Ben and Martin about today's plan.

"I was thinking last night in bed and 1 think we should find out more about this guy before we decide if we're going to confront him or not," Martin said as he sipped a cup of coffee.

"I think 1 can help you there too," Ben began. "I have a friend here that's into the Occult and might know a fair bit about Robert Darkfall or this Joshua guy."

Martin thought for a moment and then said, "Alright, but I want you to take David with you, I'm not letting you go anywhere by yourself anymore. I want to go to the city police and see if they'll let me use their files to find out about these guys."

David quickly looked at Martin, for a moment he thought about telling him he didn't want to have anything to do with visiting anyone who was involved in the Occult. He quickly dismissed the idea, telling himself that Jesus would be by his side. He understood why Martin wanted them to go as a team, and a part of David was pleased that he had become a protector, of sorts.

He looked at Ben, who was searching a phone book for the number of his friend. He wondered if it was right for them to be going to people who were involved in the very thing that they were fighting against, to get help. David wasn't sure if it was right but he put the thought aside, telling himself, if it was wrong God would have His way in the end.

"Found it," Ben said. He picked up the phone and dialed the number. A moment later a man's voice said, "Good day."

"Hello, Damien. How are you?" Ben said. His voice seemed to have a different edge to it now.

"Gideon! Is it you?" Damien asked happily.

"It is, though I go by my given name now. I've become a Christian, Damien," Ben stated.

"My, my. How things change," Damien said, amused. "How can I be of service to an old practitioner of the dark arts?"

"I need to meet with you."

"Where?"

"Your house is fine. Say in an hour?" Ben knew that he was giving Damien the home advantage. But he also knew that he had Jesus on his side.

"I will be waiting."

"I will be bringing a friend."

"Very well." Then Damien hung up the phone.

As Ben put the phone on the cradle, Martin looked confused. "What was that all about?" he asked.

"What?" Ben replied.

"It sounded like you were playing word games with him," David said.

"I was," Ben said. "You see, he wants us to think that he's in control. So he tries to get information out of us so that he can use it later." Ben stood and walked into the kitchen, David and Martin followed.

"So what I did was I gave him an advantage, I said we'd meet him at his house. Basically, that's the place where he can draw the most power," Ben said as he poured himself a glass of orange juice. "That didn't bother me all that much because we have a stronger force on our side." Ben sat down and sipped leisurely at his drink.

"I don't understand this information thing," David said as he sat beside Ben.

"Well, the simple explanation is, information is power in this subculture," Ben started.

Marianne walked into the kitchen and went to the fridge to pour herself a drink. "Information is what??" she asked casually.

"Information is power in the Magick subculture," David said with a smile. "I thought everyone knew that."

"Anyway," Ben continued with a chuckle. "If he can find out from us why we want to know about Joshua and Robert, he will have something they will need."

"What are you talking about?" Marianne asked as she sat at the table.

"Ben and I are going to talk with an old friend of his about the guys we're here to investigate," David supplied.

"Is he involved in the Occult too?" Marianne asked.

Ben nodded his head, "He's a Wiccan. If these guys are as big as they seem in the Magick circles then he'll know about them."

"What's a Wiccan?" Marianne asked.

Ben leaned back in his seat. "Wiccan is a non-violent Occult practice. They worship nature and trees and such."

"It still doesn't make it right," David said. Ben nodded and smiled in return.

"Is it safe?" Marianne asked, thinking about Ben's last encounter with the Occult.

"Yes," Ben said with a reassuring smile. "Damien's just a follower. He plays at being more than that but in the end he doesn't lead anything."

"Well, you two should get ready to go to your meeting, I'll drop you off there on my way to the police station," Martin said from where he leaned on the counter. Then he looked at Marianne. "Are you and the others going to the library today?" he asked.

"No. Christine said she wanted to talk to me about some stuff so we're going out to lunch," Marianne replied. "Mike was talking about going, but he's not even up yet."

"Well, guys," Martin said. "Looks like it's just the three of us today."

The three of them piled into Collette's van and Martin drove them to the address they received from the phone book. Ben and David stood in front of the apartment building and stared at each other for a moment. Ben wasn't sure if David was feeling well.

"You OK?" Ben asked.

David pulled himself out of the strange trance he was in. "Yeah ... you?" he said unconvincingly.

"You sure you want to come in here?" Ben asked.

"Yeah, I'll be fine," David replied with a deep breath.

The two walked into the old, run-down apartment and made their way to the basement floor. They passed aged stained doors and dirty children that were playing in the halls half nude. They heard a man and a woman arguing loudly behind one of the doors and then passed a strange symbol painted on one of the walls.

"This building is a Wiccan Coven. Sometimes the larger covens can actually manage to buy up most of the apartments in a building and that way, they can have a place to practice their ceremonies," Ben said to David in a matter-of-fact tone. "Unfortunately, these kids end up growing up in this environment and never learn of Christ until they've been so brainwashed by the coven that it's next to impossible to get them out."

"Don't the police get involved in this?" David asked.

"It's not illegal to practice witchcraft," Ben replied. "It's a recognized religion."

David huffed in disgust.

They reached a door with a strange symbol on the front, that Ben didn't recognize. He paused for a moment and wondered what Damien was up to.

"You follow me, OK?" he said to David.

David nodded, the tension was starting to build in his stomach. He looked at the door and had to overcome a sudden urge to vomit.

Ben knocked strongly on the door. A moment later it opened and Damien stood before them.

Damien stood about 6'3" and was large. David looked at him and saw him as a huge oak tree that seemed immovable. He had a long mop of curly brown hair on his head that constantly got in his eyes, which pierced out and seemed to penetrate into David's very soul with a brilliant, bright blue.

"Gideon," Damien said with a pleasant tenor voice.

"Damien," Ben responded, then he turned to David. "This is David, my friend."

"And mine." Damien bowed slightly in David's direction.

There was an awkward moment of silence, then Damien turned and said suddenly, "Enter freely and unafraid."

Ben smiled and walked into Damien's living room. The furniture was designed for effectiveness rather than style. The couch didn't match with the chair and the coffee table was just a large wooden box that Damien himself had made.

Ben smiled and sat down on the couch, David sat beside him, the sudden urge to vomit had gotten worse when they entered the room.

"Can I fix you some tea?" Damien asked.

"No, thank you, we can't stay long," Ben replied.

"It must be important, Gideon, if you can't spend some time to enjoy my hospitality. Your manners are lacking," Damien chastised.

"They always did, didn't they?" Ben responded.

Damien nodded. "What may I do for you, then; since you are in a hurry."

"We need to know about a man you should know," Ben began. "His name is Robert Darkfall."

Damien stared for a moment at Ben before he pulled his eyes away. "Why do you wish to know of him?" he asked.

"That is our business," Ben said. "You have no need to know that."

"If I am to give you the information you require, then yes, I do need to know why," Damien replied, locking his eyes with Ben's.

"We are in search of him, because he has certain information we need," Ben said.

Damien watched Ben a bit longer, as if deciding whether or not his answer was the full truth. Then he turned and walked toward the window.

"Robert Darkfall is the Superior of the Cult of Ctchutic." He paused and looked back at Ben with a smile. "You should know all about that cult." Then he turned back to the window. "As far as I know he is a hard leader who leans more toward the more violent aspects of his chosen daemon. I also know he has some sort of link with Joshua Smith, the Concierge of the Cult of Siggurath. Robert also has some sort of interest in a girl, in your home town, although I don't know what or who."

David jerked his head toward Ben. What was that? he thought. Robert has an interest in one of the girls? Who could it be? What if it was Marianne? The thought frightened David more than he could ever remember being frightened before.

Ben regarded David's expression, then noticed Damien had stopped talking. He looked back at the big man standing by the window and said, "Do you know the addresses of these people?"

Damien turned and smiled at Ben, "Why do you want Joshua's address, Gideon?"

Ben smiled, "Because you deemed it important to tell us about him, so I thought we'd pay him a visit too."

Damien's smile faded. "You can find Robert at 13645 West Bruce Avenue. And you can reach Joshua at 1784 Jordan Street."

Ben stood, and walked to Damien. "Thank you, Damien. You have been an invaluable source of information."

Damien strode over and stood in front of Ben, towering over him.

For a moment David thought he was going to strike Ben, who stood calmly staring into the large man's eyes.

"Tell me, Gideon. Do you ever miss the power?" Damien asked. "Do you ever miss the feeling of being one with the universe? Do you ever miss the knowledge that you, are a part of the power that keeps the universe together?"

Ben stared into Damien's eyes and smiled softly. "No, Damien, because I'm one with the being that created the universe, and the power that runs it."

Damien's eyes became hard and he stared down at Ben with hatred.

"Remember, Damien. You invited us into your house. We are your guests," Ben said harshly.

"You must go now."

Ben smiled and bowed slightly before he turned to move toward the door. David stood and followed in a slight daze, confused over what had just transpired. Damien opened the door for them and watched them walk down the hall until they started up the stairs.

After he closed the door, Damien went immediately to his telephone. He dialed a number and waited for an answer.

"Good day," Raven's voice said over the receiver.

"Raven, it's Damien. I just had an interesting visit from Gideon. What is it he's after?" Damien asked.

"What did he want to know?"

"He was asking about Robert and Joshua."

"What did you tell him?"

"What does he want, Raven?" Damien pressed.

"Remember your place, Wicca. I have more power than you will ever achieve. What did you tell him?" Raven said angrily.

Damien faltered a bit before answering. "I told him nothing, simply addresses."

"Did you tell him who Robert really is?" Raven asked suddenly.

"No. Should 1 have?"

"No." Then Raven hung up the phone.

In Windsor, Raven stood in front of a wall covered in framed pictures. He stood for a long time staring in the same spot, at the same picture. It was a picture with no glass in the frame, of two young men standing in front of a waterfall.

"What became of us?" Raven asked the picture over and over.

David and Ben stood on the street thinking about their next move. David started to feel a bit better after they left the building and was searching the street for a cab.

"You seemed kind of nervous in there," Ben said. "You OK now?"

David nodded, concentrating on his self-employed task.

"Bruce Avenue is only a couple of blocks away, why don't we just walk it?" Ben offered.

David looked over at Ben with a tired expression and then nodded. "OK, that sounds good," he said with a forced smile.

Ben paused for a moment and looked at David critically. His eyes were drawn and tired looking with large dark circles under them. His hair, which he normally kept carefully brushed and styled, was unkempt and rolling over his shoulders.

"Do you just want to go home?" Ben asked.

David shook his head. "No, I want to know about this Joshua guy," he said emphatically.

"Look, David I'm sure that Damien was just trying to scare us in there," Ben said.

David looked at Ben hardly. "What if he wasn't."

"David, you're losing your objectivity. The cultists are starting to get to you. You can't let your personal feelings get involved in this, they'll use them against you," Ben retorted.

"And what if it was Sara?" David said softly.

"Then I'd have to deal with it. But we don't know who it is or if it's even true." Ben's eyes softened and he continued, "Look, 1 don't like the idea any more than you do. But we both have to deal with it. We can't give them anything to use on us."

David slowly nodded his head, and they started up the street, David's shoulders bowed as if under a tremendous weight. Ben followed closely, starting to seriously worry about his stocky, strong friend, who at this moment seemed more of a lost child.

Martin walked into the Toronto police station and asked to speak to the Captain. When asked what the business was he simply flashed his badge and the uniformed officer walked into the office to speak to the Captain. A moment later he came out and said the Captain would see him in a moment.

Martin waited in the foyer about ten minutes until the Captain opened the door to his office and invited Martin in.

The office was small and cramped. Sheaves of paper covered the desk, and the Captain, who was a mid-sized man of about forty-five, sat down behind his desk and straightened his neatly knotted tie.

"How can 1 help you, Detective ... ?" the Captain began.

"Martin, sir," was the reply. "I am here to get information on some people whom we believe to be involved in two murders in Windsor."

The Captain leaned back in his chair and pulled a cigarette out of a gold case and laid the case on his desk. Martin glanced down at the case, momentarily admiring its craftsmanship. He noticed an engraving on the top and then he took a sharp breath of air. It was the same symbol that was on the walls of the churches in Windsor.

The Captain noticed the breath, looked at the case, then at Martin. "Is something wrong, Martin?" he asked, as he replaced the case to his inside jacket pocket.

"No, sir. I'm just getting over a cold and cigarette smoke bothers me a bit," Martin lied.

"What are the names of the people you're looking for?"

Martin thought for a moment, "Robert Darkfall."

The Captain stood and walked toward the door to the office and called a uniformed officer to him.

"Take the detective to the records room," he said. Then he turned to Martin. "You can look through any records you want."

"Thank you, sir," Martin said as he quickly followed the officer to a room marked RECORDS.

Just as Martin thought; there was nothing in the files on Robert Darkfall, not even a parking ticket. Martin slammed the file shut and stood staring at the wall for a moment. He decided to return to the house and think about what his next move should be.

As Martin walked out of the station he turned and noticed that the Captain he spoke with was watching him leave.

Christine and Marianne stepped out of a restaurant on Bay street and into the cold air.

"I'll spring for a cab back to Collette's," Marianne said with a toss of her blond hair.

They stood at the curb for a few moments before a large black car pulled up along side them. The back door opened and a man stepped out and said, "Miss Marianne Storm?"

Marianne stood in confusion for a moment before she replied. "Yes, who are you?"

"Robert Darkfall, Miss Storm," was the reply.

"Robert what?" Marianne replied, shocked.

Before either girl could recover from the statement the man quickly, and forcefully, ushered them into the awaiting vehicle.

"What are you doing?" Marianne asked angrily as the car sped down the street.

"We're taking you to see Mr. Smith."

"What for?" Marianne replied.

"We'll see," was the cold answer.

# Chapter Nine

Thirteen-six-forty-five West Bruce Street was a small house in the middle of a crowded street. Stores and restaurants sat around the building abundance.

"Well, here we are. At the end of the search," David said quietly.

"We think. We still have to talk to this guy and see if he has any connection with the murders," Ben replied. He stepped up to the door and knocked loudly.

They stood in silence for a few moments, staring at the huge oaken door. Then, just as they were about to turn away, the doorknob turned and a gaunt man stood before them, looking blankly out in the sunlight.

"What can I do for you?" the man asked, distractedly. He stared out at Ben and David, as if their very existence surprised him.

David looked the man up and down, then smiled shyly and looked away when he noticed the man's fly was down. When David pointed at the problem the man casually reached down and corrected it.

Ben smiled and cleared his throat, causing the man to turn in his direction.

"Excuse me, sir," Ben began. "We're looking for Robert Darkfall."

The gaunt man stepped back and smiled stupidly. "You must be his friends from the other group," he slurred. "He said you'd be coming to see him. Come on in." The man opened the door wider in an inviting way, then stood confused when David and Ben didn't enter.

"Is Robert here?" David asked.

The man shook his head. "No. He went to talk to another leader."

"Who?" Ben pressed.

"Joshua Smith. He's the Concierge of Siggurath." Then the man waved his arm in. "You coming or not?"

"No," Ben replied. "We'll just go talk to Robert at Smith's place."

The man shrugged and closed the door, leaving David and Ben standing on the porch alone again.

"What was wrong with him?" David asked as they left the yard.

"Doped up," Ben answered. "Maybe he was just in a trance-state. I'd say doped though because he was so open about the cults."

"Where to now?" David asked. "Smith's?" David spat out the name like it was a bad taste in his mouth. Ben stopped and turned to face his friend.

"Yes. Smith's," he replied. "But first you have to get control of your feelings. You pray while we walk."

The walk was long and pleasant in the early afternoon air. A light breeze blew up the street and cooled them down but didn't make it uncomfortable. They walked through the streets, the crunching of the snow the only other sound, each hiding their own thoughts from the other.

Ben had the same fears as David, that this man might be after Marrianne for some reason. Ben knew that sometimes the cults could get violent about keeping their secrets but how could the Siggurath cult know about the girls, and why was it that they were after them and not Ben. Normally they would go after ex-cult members so they would be a lesson to others. And why was there a nagging voice in the back of his head warning him of this man, and what he wants?

That voice that had saved his life so many times. That voice that warned of danger. Why was it screaming now?

David's thoughts were only of Marianne. He had tried to pray, but like every other time in the past few weeks, he couldn't concentrate. He worried about her and what this man might represent to her. What would he do if this man tried to kill her? He knew the answer to that question. He would stand by her until his death if need be. He wouldn't let her stand alone against anything if he could help her.

They arrived at 1784 Jordan Street at about 12:30. The house was small and nondescript. It seemed like any other house that lined the quiet tree shaded street. Ben walked up to the large metal door and knocked heavily on it.

David's heart pounded in his chest, and he felt that it would burst forth and fall onto the ground like a fish out of water. David felt a sudden well of anger come out of the depths of his belly. He wanted suddenly to kill this man named Joshua Smith. This man that thought he could end the lives of people, simply because they were different than himself. Simply because he had the power. That a worthless thing that worshiped Satan could ever touch something beautiful in this world was beyond belief. David wanted to kill this man named Joshua Smith, because he made David want to kill.

The door opened, and before them stood a man about six feet tall and of average build for a man in his late forties. His short, neatly cut hair was graying about the temples and his crisp blue eyes peered out at them gently from behind bifocals.

"May I help you?" the man asked.

David was beyond words, he simply stood in surprise at the man. Ben paused for a moment then said, "Yes, we're looking for Joshua Smith."

The man smiled then replied, "You've found him. How can 1 help you?"

Marianne and Christine were driven to the same small house. They were taken inside, via the garage and down into the basement, where they were deposited roughly into a small room with chairs and a cot. The door slammed behind them and the room was blanketed in a thick, black darkness the girls felt they could touch, or that could touch them.

After a few moments, Christine started to cry. Marianne walked over to her and placed her arms about the frightened girl and held her close.

"Everything will be alright, Chrissy. You'll see," Marianne said in her most reassuring tone.

"I don't understand, Marianne. Why are we here?" Christine said between sobs.

"I don't know," Marianne replied as they sat on the cot. "But I'm sure someone around here has some answers to give us."

Christine lifted her head from Marianne's shoulder and looked at her through the darkness.

"What are they going to do with us?" she asked tentatively.

Marianne bowed her head and looked at her feet through the darkness. "I don't know," she said softly. "But I do know that God is on our side and as long as we have faith in him we'll be fine." Marianne grasped Christine's hand tightly.

Christine looped her arm into Marianne's. "What do they want with us?" she asked.

"I don't know," was the simple reply.

Ben and David stood in front of Joshua Smith, confused. They didn't understand why he looked so different than any of the other Occult members they had seen in the past. They were not prepared for this kind of a person.

"Sir, my name is Ben Steele and this is David Masterson, we're involved in an investigation from Windsor and we'd like to ask you a few questions," Ben said after a moment of awkward silence.

Joshua stepped back and moved aside from the door. David started to move forward but was suddenly stopped by Ben's hand on his shoulder.

"We haven't been invited in, David. Where are your manners?"

Ben said. He felt the common sense coming back after the initial shock of seeing Joshua for the first time.

Joshua turned and studied Ben for a long time before saying, "Are you police?"

"No," Ben replied. "Are you afraid?"

"No," Joshua smiled. "Should I be?"

"No," Ben said softly.

"Very well then, my friends," Joshua suddenly became more animated, and opened the door wider. "Enter freely and unafraid!"

Joshua's house was just as confusing as Joshua's appearance. It was neatly decorated with paintings of grassy landscapes and wildlife. A plush living room set dominated the front room of his small house. As Ben looked around the small room he noticed a set of stairs leading down into a basement area.

That's most likely where he has his ceremonies, Ben thought to himself. I wonder how we're going to get down there?

"Would you like some coffee, or tea perhaps?" Joshua said pleasantly.

"No, thank you," Ben replied. "I would like to ask you some questions about the cult of Ctchutic."

Joshua's eyes widened ever so slightly then returned to the smiling state they had been in. He sat down on the plush couch and motioned to the other chairs in the room and smiled.

"Very well," he said quietly.

Ben and David sat in the chairs and Ben leaned forward to ask his questions.

"What do you know about Robert Darkfall?"

"I know that he is a man that holds a great deal of power in the Occult circles, Mr. Steele," Joshua replied. Then he added. "Now, why do you want to know about him? Quid pro quo, Mr Steele."

Ben looked up at Joshua and met his eyes for a moment, there was nothing there, he saw. No life at all.

"He's part of the investigation that we're involved in. We want to know everything you know about him," Ben replied carefully.

Joshua leaned forward and locked eyes with Ben. "Are you willing to tell me everything you know about your investigation?" he said with a smile, knowing the answer.

"No," Ben said softly.

Joshua suddenly stood up and laughed, "I didn't think so, Mr. Steele, or may I call you Gideon?"

Ben's head shot up and caught Joshua's eyes in a lock of hate for a brief second before they faded to surprise. He stood and faced the tall man for a moment, behind him, he heard David stand up and come to his side.

"Surprised you, did IT' Joshua said. "Well, yes, 1 do know all about your investigation, and yes, 1 do know who you are. I know who you all are. A group of university students who are doing the right thing in God's eyes by helping a pathetic excuse for a cop investigate a murder of a priest and a pastor." Joshua laughed again for a moment and removed his glasses. "That really is something." He walked to the door and opened it. "You should leave now, I have guests."

Ben walked to the door and stopped in front of Joshua.

"We'll be back for you. And we'll win," Ben said.

"I wouldn't be so sure of that, my friend. You'll be thinking that on the outside of this door," Joshua replied coldly. "You're trying my hospitality, leave."

The door slammed shut behind them and Ben had to repress the urge to swear loudly. He let Joshua walk all over him in that house. He couldn't believe Joshua had all but confessed to being involved in the murders. Not with words but with actions. He knew about the investigation. Why? He knew about the university students. Why? He knew about Martin. Why? The questions just kept piling up, and no answers for them.

"I don't understand what just happened in there but I didn't like it," David said with a glare back at the house.

"Well, I do understand what just happened and I didn't like it one bit, my friend," Ben replied. "I just wish I knew what he was hiding."

David turned and stopped at the end of the short walkway in front of the house. "What do you mean hiding?" he asked in awe. "He all but confessed to being involved in the murders!"

"I know that, David," Ben replied with a grimace. "But there was something else. Something I couldn't put my finger on."

David shrugged his shoulders and looked up the street to a phone booth.

"We should call and check in," David said.

Ben nodded and followed his stocky friend to the booth where he called Collette's house. After a moment David's face went ashen and he looked back at Joshua's house with undisguised hatred. Ben stepped in front of him as he left the booth and started back toward the house.

"What's up?" Ben asked.

David glared up at Ben and locked eyes with him. There was a moment, a brief moment when David thought to strike out at Ben to remove him from the path that David had chosen. But when he locked eyes with Ben, he found the ice blue eyes held a faith in the abilities that Ben had honed to perfection, and that if David were to try those abilities he would find himself on the short end of the deal.

"He has Marianne," David spat out between clenched teeth. "We have to go help her."

Ben thought for a moment, and looked back at the house that held so many secrets, and he wanted to find the answers.

"How do you know that he has her?" Ben asked, not taking his eyes from the house.

"Collette said that Marianne called, and said she was with her Uncle

Joshua. Ben, Marianne doesn't have an Uncle Joshua. Maybe we should just say Joshua Smith." David said as he moved up beside Ben.

"We can go in there. Can't we?"

Ben looked down at his stocky friend and smiled weakly, "No, we can't. They'd kill us both in a second." David started to speak but Ben cut him off, "As much as I love Marianne I'm not about to do anything stupid right now." Ben looked up the street to a small coffee shop.

"Call Collette back and tell her to get Sara, Mike and Martin to meet us at that coffee shop. As soon as possible." Then Ben started back toward the phone booth. "We'll think there. At least if he moves we can move with him."

David nodded absently and threw a withering glare at the house before turning to call Collette. After the call, the two young men walked to the coffee shop on the corner of the quiet street where Joshua Smith lived.

Ben chose a seat where they could see the house, and observe what was happening. David ordered two coffees for them, and sat down across from his friend.

David's mind was filtering through thousands of ideas as he sipped slowly at his coffee. He dreaded to think of some of the things that might be happening to Marianne in that cursed house across the street. David's hands slowly curled into tightly clenched fists as he thought of Joshua Smith having possession of the girl he loved.

Ben reached out across the table and slapped David's hands.

"Stop that!" he scolded. "There's no need to think violence. We have the situation under control right now as best as we can."

"You could go in there and get her out, couldn't you?" David asked as he placed his hands in his lap.

"Yes, possibly, but I won't."

"Why?" David demanded.

"Because I'm thinking clearly and you aren't," Ben replied. David's brow furrowed with confusion for a moment, then he looked directly at Ben. "Christine was with her!" he exclaimed. "They went out for lunch didn't they?"

Ben nodded. "One person in the house would be no real problem to sneak out but two is a bit touchy. And I'm not really up to par from my last run in with this cult yet."

David glared at Ben. "But what if it was Sara, then what would you do?"

Ben thought for a moment. "Probably the same thing we're doing. Just cause I'm in love with her, it doesn't give me the right to lose my good sense. The best thing we can do is keep thinking with a clear head." Then Ben looked critically at David. "What if it was Collette and Christine?"

David looked at his coffee mug with a beaten expression. "1 suppose you're right," he finally said.

Ben and David sat in silence for a few minutes before Ben looked out at the house.

A large van had pulled up to the side of the house and two men were loading something large onto it. Joshua stood nearby directing the men with short, curt instructions and then climbed into the driver's seat.

Ben stood and motioned David to follow him outside. At that moment, Martin and the others pulled up in Collette's bright red van and opened the side door for Ben and David.

"Follow that van!" Ben said as he pointed out Joshua's vehicle.

"Hello to you too," Martin grumbled as he pulled out of the coffee shop's parking lot.

"What's going on?" Mike asked as he helped David into a seat.

"Joshua just loaded some stuff into that van and we want to know where he's going," David answered.

"What do you think it is?" Sara asked from behind Ben.

"I'm not sure but 1 think they're moving the girls somewhere else," Ben answered.

"You mean you think Christine's with them too?" Mike asked in horror. "How?"

"Well, she was with Marianne, Mike," Martin said as he turned the van down a long empty road. "Where does this go?" he asked Collette, who sat in the passenger seat.

"This goes to the airport," Collette replied. "Why would he go here?"

"Collette, do you have a phone in here?" Ben asked.

"Yeah, there's a cellular in the cabinet beside you."

"Thanks." Ben pulled out the phone and called information to get a number for the airport. Then he called the airport.

"Yes, I'd like the engineering department please," Ben said to the pleasant sounding voice that answered. After a moment a low bass voice answered the incessant ring.

"Engineering."

"Steve? It's Ben."

"Hi, Ben. How are you?" Steve replied happily.

"Not too good. Can I meet you in the parking lot by the ticket booths in a few minutes?" Ben said.

"You're here? In Toronto?"

"In a few?" Ben persisted.

"Yeah, sure."

Then Ben hung up.

"Steve? What do we need Steve for?" David asked.

Ben turned to look at David. "Hopefully we won't, but if Joshua's up to what 1 think he is we might need a plane," he answered.

"Steve's not a pilot," Sara said.

"No, but between the two of us we should be able to figure it out," Ben smiled.

Martin groaned, "I don't hear this! You're talking about stealing a plane, and flying without a license, from an international airport no less! That could danger thousands of lives!"

"Steve's working on experimental airplanes as part of his engineering degree from the University of Toronto. It's his job to see that they operate safely," Ben explained. "If God is with us, we may meet another friend of mine that flies out of Toronto. That way we'll have a real pilot."

"Jamie?" Collette asked as they stopped in front of a tall lanky man in a white lab coat with scores of pens in the pocket.

"Yep," Ben answered as he jumped out of the van and shook hands with the tall man.

In a moment, the entire group was gathered around their old friend and shaking hands or hugging him, which made him appear uncomfortable.

"Steve, this is a new friend of ours, Martin. Martin, Steve," David said.

After shaking hands with the large detective, Steve turned to Ben.

"What's going on?" he asked simply.

Ben smiled. "Well, David walked past Assumption church and found out that there was a murder there and then he came to us and we went to the church to see if we could help, but I didn't want to go at first, then I changed my mind. It turned out that it was an Occult thing and the priest that was killed was trying to raise daemons, not a very priestly thing to do eh? Anyway, while David and I were doing that the others, Sara, Marianne and Mike were at the library finding stuff out, they found out that the priest was involved in some kind of a debate with a bunch of cult leaders and the cult leaders came out on the short end of the stick. Anyway then we went home and then we talked to Martin some more and then there was another murder, so David and I went to that one too and found a kind of symbol type thing. Then I went to an old friend of mine and David went home. Then I got shot at and was brought home by someone that didn't leave any footprints, and then Martin came to us and said that we should go to Toronto to check out this Joshua Smith guy, anyway then we came here and talked to Joshua who kidnapped Marianne and Christine and we followed them here and we think he's going to leave by plane and we need your help. And do you know if Jamie's here?"

Steve stared at Ben like he had grown another head. Then he slowly looked at the others in turn to see if they were laughing. When he saw they weren't, he looked back at Ben and grunted softly.

"So this Joshua guy is trying to leave by plane with Marianne and Christine?" Steve asked.

"I don't believe it. He got all that!" Martin exclaimed.

"I've known him for a while," Steve replied.

"Yeah, we think," Ben answered.

Steve grunted again. "Come with me." Steve led them along the outside of the building and around to where the planes were taxing, preparing for takeoff.

"There's the van!" David yelled, pointing to where Joshua was overseeing the movement of two long rectangular boxes.

"This could just be me, but I wonder if those are big enough to put people in?" Steve asked.

David looked up at the tall man and said, "You don't think he would do that, do you?"

Ben thought for a moment. "Why would he put them in boxes? If he was moving them in North America they could just ride in seats, as long as they could prove they were Canadian."

Steve looked at the large cargo plane the boxes were being loaded onto. "Unless Marianne's changed a great deal, I can't see her being quiet about being kidnapped," he said softly. "That plane could easily make it anywhere in the North Western Hemisphere on one refuel. That's a big area to look for two people."

"We need a plane," Ben said.

"You need a brain!" Steve replied. "You think I can just give you a plane and a full tank of fuel?"

"Steve! We have to help Marianne and Christine," David pleaded. "Please."

"Who would fly it?" Steve asked.

"Is Jamie here?" Ben replied.

"Jamie has his own plane now." Steve thought for a moment. "I'll tell you what. If Jamie will fly you guys, I'll get you a free tank of fuel."

"How big is his plane?" Martin asked.

"It'll only hold six," Steve said. "So only two of you will be able to go, because I'll have to navigate."

Martin looked at Steve and then at Ben. "You and David go." Sara started to say something and then Martin cut her off. "No, Sara, I'm not going to go. I have a job here, and I can't just up and take off out of the country. David's going to argue that he's going whether I say yes or no, and I want Ben there to make sure David, Marianne and Christine stay alive." Then he turned to Ben. "1 want you to be sure to get the girls out safely and if at all possible use the police.

"The others and I will be working on getting evidence to arrest Joshua and Robert when they get back here." Then Martin turned his large frame to David. "You listen to Ben, he knows this subculture better than you do, so he's in charge. Agreed?"

David nodded soberly.

"I think we'd better go and find Jamie," Steve said.

"We've also have to find out where that plane is going," David replied, turning to the plane that Joshua was getting into. "Its registration number is

CHQ 145."

"That shouldn't be a problem."

Steve led the small group into the large hanger and past many odd and strange looking planes, through a secured door that he opened with a small plastic card, and into a room filled with men and women drinking coffee and talking loudly.

One of the men, a middle sized man with blond tightly curled hair and a large friendly smile stood and made his way toward them.

"Ben!" he said loudly and stuck out his hand to grasp Ben's tightly. "How are you?"

"Not bad, Jamie. I'm glad to see you're here," Ben replied.

Jamie looked doubtful and a scowl creased his face. "What do you want?"

Ben smiled and quickly related the information he'd passed on to Steve a few minutes before.

After he was finished Jamie smiled back and laughed. "That sounds like a pretty hairy adventure. And now you need a pilot to follow this guy where ever he's going, right?"

Ben nodded.

"And immediately your good friend Jamie popped into your head as a swell guy to fly his plane all over creation to find the girls, right?"

Ben smiled and nodded.

Jamie smiled back and looked out toward the hanger. "That's a mighty sweet plane 1 have now, 1 call her The Skyhawk." Then his brow furrowed in thought again. "Where are we going?"

Steve smiled, "We don't know yet, I was just going to call up to the tower and find out." Then he moved to a phone on the wall and dialed a number. "I'll give you a free filling of fuel for the trip," he said as he waited for an answer.

"1 like that idea," Jamie smiled. "How have you guys been?"

Jamie asked.

Sara smiled, "Not bad, except for this, of course."

Mike nodded and said, "I wish I could go with you guys."

"Yeah, who's going anyway? The Skyhawk only seats six and we'll need the extra seats for Marianne and Christine," Jamie said.

"Ben, David and Steve," Sara said sadly

Ben gave her a tight hug. "We'll be fine." Then he turned to Martin.

"Why don't you take them home now. We can handle this from here."

Martin nodded. "Good luck."

Ben smiled slyly. "We don't need luck, we have Jesus."

After a short goodbye, Martin and Collette left to wait in the van.

Mike took Ben's hand firmly.

"Bring her back safe, please," he said, barely able to hold back his tears.

Ben smiled as reassuringly as he could. "We'll do our best, Mike." As Mike went to say goodbye to David, Sara kissed Ben softly on the lips and whispered in his ear, "I love you."

Ben held her close to him, enjoying the warmth of her body and whispered back, "I know, Blossom. I'll see you soon."

Mumbling a teary goodbye to David, Sara and Mike went to meet the others in the parking lot.

Steve returned and motioned for the three remaining friends to follow him.

"Well, they're staying in Canada," Steve said. "They're registered as going on a flight over James Bay and then landing in one of the surrounding public landing strips."

"What??" Ben said, as he ducked under the wing of a plane.

"That's going to make it really hard to nail them down," Jamie said.

"We have to get up in the air now!" David yelled. "Who knows what could happen if they get on the ground and we don't know where they are?!"

Jamie lifted his hand. "I understand that, David. That's why we're going to get up as soon as possible and track them. We'll follow just above and to the right of them. They won't be able to see us."

"We didn't bring any clothes," David said.

"We're not going on vacation," Ben replied. "We'll most likely be there only two days at the most. Besides we've got plastic if we need anything."

Jamie smiled. "Ah yes! Just like the old days. No plans, no clues, and no brain. Don't you ever change, Ben?"

Ben smiled, "Can we talk about this in the sky?"

After a few moments, Steve led the three men to a middle sized plane that was painted black and sported twin propeller engines. Jamie climbed into the cockpit and after a few moments of looking, declared he was ready for take-off. Ben took the left seat, while Steve sat in a chair with communications instruments and engine monitors and a computer screen in front of him. David sat in a passenger seat beside Steve, feeling a little left out, but realizing that with his mind on Marianne he would be little help until they got to James Bay anyway.

"This is Skyhawk II, cross country flight to James Bay area. Requesting clearance to takeoff," Steve said into his headset.

After a moment, the tower replied with the clearance and that the runway was clear.

The take-off was smooth, and as Jamie brought the plane around,

Steve mentioned he could spot Joshua's plane on his radar. Ben looked down at the ground and marveled at the sight of the snow covered fields that surrounded Toronto, like a delicately painted portrait of the glory of God.

David remained quiet through most of the flight, the anger at Marianne's kidnapping not so much pain now as it was an annoying fact that David was determined to correct. The most remarkable thing David noticed, however, wasn't that he loved Marianne enough to go after her, it was that he had finally admitted to himself that he had no control over what happened to himself or to Marianne and that it was the Lord's will that ruled his life.

As David sat in the passenger seat behind Jamie, he looked out the window to the clouds beyond and gave total control of his life to God. Shortly after that, he fell asleep and was blanketed in a deep, restful sleep.

# Chapter Ten

Martin drove Collette's van back to the house slowly. The sudden absence of Ben and David was felt by everyone, the ride was quiet as they each thought of their own concerns.

Martin wondered if he was doing the right thing. He knew he couldn't leave the city. He had to return to work on Monday and the trip that Ben and David started would most likely take them at least until Tuesday. He could have called in sick, but that would have been against the oath he took when he received his badge. Their lives were under his protection and he let two of them go off to a potentially dangerous situation.

It was necessary, he kept on telling himself, he was certain of it.

But there was that nagging doubt in the back of his mind, pulling at him and telling him he was doing the wrong thing, he was letting Ben and David walk into their own deaths. Was he?

Sara's thoughts were only on God at this time. Praying, thanking and begging for the Lord to keep Ben, David, Jamie and Steve safe. Understandably, her thoughts and prayers were mostly on behalf of Ben but she didn't forget the others who had gone with him.

Mike was a wreck, his hands were shaking, and he had broken out in a cold sweat. Absently, he wondered what a heart attack felt like. Then he sighed and knew that it wasn’t a heart attack. It was the realization that he finally accepted the fact that he loved Christine. A fact that slapped him in the face by the thought she was in danger somewhere and he couldn't help her. Why was David allowed to go and he wasn't? Or why was Ben allowed to go? He had no romantic ties with Marianne or with Christine. Yet, Mike thought, Ben had the skills, and David was a more logical choice than Mike. David was more reserved and would think before he acted. That's what Mike felt anyway.

Collette was wondering how she had come into contact with these people. Marianne had called her the day before and asked if they could stay for the weekend, she had given Collette a quick story of what was going on but not the full picture. And now, Collette was mixed up in the kidnapping of two of her closest friends and trying to figure out the murderer of two men she had never even met. Life is strange, she thought with a smile.

They pulled into the driveway fifty minutes after they left Ben and David at the airport, not one word was spoken the entire time. Now Martin turned in his seat and looked at Mike, and Sara.

"Well, it looks like it will just be the three of us gathering proof in Windsor," he said.

Collette tapped Martin on the arm and smiled. "I've been thinking of visiting Windsor for a long time. Would now be a good time?"

Martin sighed and nodded. "The more the merrier," he said dryly.

Raven stepped off the train and scanned the faces in Union Station in Toronto. He noticed the familiar face almost immediately.

Robert Darkfall had long black hair that laid casually across his shoulders. His slightly pointed eyes gave away the fact that he was half Chinese, and his slim build fanned up toward broad, powerful shoulders.

He hasn't slept well lately, Raven thought upon seeing the dark circles under his friend and superior's eyes.

"Good evening, Raven," Robert said as he shook Raven's hand. "I trust the trip was comfortable?"

"Yes, it was, thank you, Robert," Raven replied. "I came as soon as I received Damien's call. I felt you might need me to talk to Gideon." Raven smiled. "Or if you needed me to help fix whatever else he has disrupted."

Robert's eyes narrowed, as they turned and started walking to the exit. "I need no help from you Raven," he hissed. "What Gideon is disrupting is between myself and Joshua. It is no concern of yours. Your concern is Damien."

"Damien?" Raven asked. "Why Damien?"

"Damien has been asking some interesting questions of certain people.

He has, for example, figured out that Joshua and I were involved in the murders. He has no proof, and I don't want him to get any," Robert said, leading Raven outside and to his awaiting car. "I want you to take one of my men to him and dispose of the pathetic little Wicca."

Raven stopped. "Damien? He has been a friend of ours for as long as I have been in the Order."

Robert turned on Raven and glared at him. "Damien has begun to question my decisions. He does not know why, nor would he understand why I do things." Robert spun and head for his car once more. "You would not question me, would you?"

Raven followed Robert with clenched fists. "No," he said softly.

"Also, Raven," Robert continued. "Joshua has taken Marianne and one of her friends to Timmins."

"His promise to the man there?" Raven asked.

"Yes," Robert replied. "Your University friends followed him to the airport and then left. Gideon and the stocky young man stayed behind at the airport. I'm wondering if they could have followed him to Timmins."

"Possibly," Raven said as he climbed into Robert's black BMW. "Gideon is a resourceful man."

Robert drove Raven to the apartment where Damien lived. Two men were waiting outside and they approached the car as Robert pulled up to the curb.

"Good evening, Robert," one of the men said.

"Good evening, Frank," Robert replied. "Is he in his apartment?"

"Yes, sir. He hasn't left all day."

"Good." Robert turned and allowed Frank to see Raven. "This is Raven. He is the High Priest of one of the sects in Windsor. He will be overseeing the termination of Damien."

Frank bowed respectfully to Raven and Raven inclined his head gently in response.

Frank was a well built man with large, bulging biceps and a barrel chest.

His companion was smaller but carried about himself an aura of fear which made Raven decide he was the more dangerous of the two men. He wondered for a moment if they were part of Robert's Order of if they were just hired help.

"Be quick about it, Frank," Robert said, then he smiled evilly. "But not too quick."

"Yes, sir," Frank replied with a grin.

Raven got out of the car and followed Frank into the apartment building, the other man stayed outside, presumably as a guard. They stepped over drunks sleeping in the halls, and passed doors that shed thin shafts of light from the cracks in them.

"This is the door," Frank said. Then he quickly raised his leg and kicked the door open.

"What is this?" Raven heard Damien say, but his face was hidden when Frank stepped in front of him.

Raven heard a short commotion and then all went quiet. After he decided it was safe, he entered the room. Damien's living room was a mess. The couch was tipped over and a lamp had fallen on its side with the bulb shattered all over the floor.

Damien was lying on the floor, his face bleeding and Frank's foot jammed at his throat. Raven stepped delicately to Damien, trying to avoid as much of the debris that was strewn on the floor.

"Raven!" Damien cried, his voice choked. He reached a hand up to Raven, fingers splayed."Help me! What's going on?"

"Robert has deemed you a liability, Damien. You should not have tried looking into his affairs," Raven said, he saw the shock and disbelief in Damien's face, his hand slowly lowered to the floor, but his eyes implored silently for mercy, staring at Raven. His throat was starting to close, and Raven wasn't sure how many words he had before his voice cracked from emotion. He simply added, "Good bye."

Frank looked at Raven and pulled out a long, wicked knife, a sadistic grin on his face.

Raven nodded sharply, turned, and walked out of the room. He stopped and closed his eyes when the screaming started. His clenched his shaking hands into fists and stood weeping, but he didn't stop listening. Fuel for the hatred, he thought.

Martin awoke the next morning with a plan. He ran down the stairs and was surprised to see Sara, Mike and Collette all waiting for him, and eating breakfast.

"I think I know how we can get some proof on Joshua and Darkfall," he said with a smile, as he sat and poured himself a bowl of cereal.

"How?" Mike asked. He had decided, the night before, that the best way to help was to give Martin all the assistance he could to put those two men behind bars.

"Well, the first thing we have to do is visit with Darkfall," Martin said.

"Visit him? Why?" Sara asked, surprised.

"People generally make mistakes when they know someone is onto them," Martin replied. "We just go there, ask a few questions and step back and see what happens."

"I kinda like it," Collette said with a smile. "I like the idea of the jerk getting an ulcer."

"Yeah," Martin replied. "Mike and I will go there and ask a few questions."

"What do you want us to do?" Sara asked.

"Pray," Martin said as he got up to change. "Pray a lot."

It took about an hour for Martin to take a shower and dress. By that time, Mike was on the edge of his seat waiting to go. The two of them climbed into Collette's van and raced to the address Ben provided for them before he left on the plane.

"That's it! There." Mike pointed at the same old house Ben and David visited the day before.

Martin parked the van and the two men walked to the front door of the house. Martin rapped solidly on the door and waited. A tall man with long black hair answered.

"May I help you?" he asked with a slight British accent.

"Yes, we're looking for Robert Darkfall," Martin replied, showing his police identification.

The man studied the badge and ID card for a moment before he looked back into the house and stepped onto the porch, closing the door.

"Your identification says that you are Detective Gregory Martin of the Windsor Police Department," he said.

"Yes," Martin replied. "I am, and this is Mike McIssic, he's assisting me .... "

"In an investigation of some murders of clergy in Windsor, I know," the man supplied. "My name is Raven. I know Gid ... Ben Steele."

Martin's eyes narrowed. "Yeah, Ben's mentioned you." Raven smiled softly. "Yes, I'm sure he has."

"Where's Robert Darkfall?" Martin pressed.

"He is inside," Raven said. "But you do not have to go in there. You will find nothing that will help you from him."

Martin smiled. "I'd like to find that out for myself, if you don't mind."

"Very well," Raven replied. "I will meet you at Collette's house in an hour," he added softly.

Martin was taken by surprise at the comment. "How do you know .... "

Raven lifted a hand to silence Martin and said, "I know much about you that would surprise you. I know much about your investigation that would surprise you too."

Raven opened the door again, "But you are determined to talk to Robert, aren't you?"

Martin nodded.

"Very well then, follow me," Raven replied. "Enter freely and unafraid."

The living room was dark and uninviting. The strong smell of incense filled Martin's nose as he took his first breath of tainted air. A man was sitting on the couch, a syringe and a spoon sitting beside him.

Raven glanced back at his charges and smiled. Martin was taking it all in with the observant eyes of an experienced detective. Michael, however, was startled. He's in another world, Raven thought about the big, chubby man. He felt almost sorry for him.

Raven led them to a back room that was decorated all in black. No windows sat in the walls to allow light into the room. Long black curtains covered the doors into and out of the room. Sitting on a large black leather chair was Robert - dressed in his customary black and petting an orange tabby cat.

"Greetings, Detective Martin, and Mr. McIssic," Robert said cordially.

"Hello," Martin replied. "I'd like to ask you a few questions."

"About what?" Robert asked.

"About two murders I'm investigating in Windsor."

"May I see some identification?" The cat jumped off Robert's lap and ran off into another room.

Martin again pulled out his identification, and showed it to Robert.

"Very well," Robert said after a long study of the badge. "How may I help you?"

"I'd like to know if you were in Windsor at any time over the past week," Martin said.

"I travel a great deal to visit the other sects of my cult I may have been there," Robert replied.

"Is there any way you can be sure?" Martin pressed.

"I will have my planner for last week sent to you in Windsor," Robert said.

"Do you have any connections with Joshua Smith?" Martin asked, watching Robert's face carefully.

Robert smiled and stroked the struggling mustache on his lip. "I believe I do have connections with him," he said. "He is the Concierge of the Cult of Siggurath, isn't he?"

"You tell me," Martin replied.

"Well, I think he is," Robert said with a tone of finality. "Unless you have a search warrant, our interview is completed." Then he stood and left the room.

"Sweet guy," Martin mumbled.

"I shall lead you to the door," Raven said quietly.

When they reached the front door, Raven grabbed Martin and turned him around, saying, "He was playing with you in there. Put no trust in anything he says, he is the Prince of Lies." Then he turned and reentered the house.

After they reached the van, Martin slammed his fist into the door.

"Relax, Martin," Mike said softly. "We'll get him. Remember, Raven is coming to Collette's, he might be willing to help us."

"Why would he do that?" Martin asked, rubbing his now sore hand.

"The way Ben explained it to me once is that the only way to advance once you have power is to get rid of the person above you. Sending Robert to jail would be a great way for Raven to advance, wouldn't it?"

"Great," Martin said dryly. "We're going to help an Occultist in order to put another one behind bars."

# Chapter Eleven

They had given her something to drink, she remembered, forcing it down her throat, then she fell asleep. Now as she opened her eyes, it was dark and cramped. She heard voices around her, someone was saying something about being careful not to hurt something. She couldn't make them out very well.

Then there was a banging, and Marianne knew she was in a box.

They were going to bury her alive! That must be it, they drugged her, locked her in this box and now they were lowering her into the hole to bury her. Suddenly the small box was filled with light as the lid came off. Two hands grabbed her roughly and pulled her into the sun. The first thing she noticed was the cold, much colder than Toronto. Then, as her eyes adjusted she saw the scores of men and women standing around her. Joshua Smith walked up to her and took her hand gently, the two men that had pulled her out of her prison box released their hold on her after a stem look from Smith. Joshua ushered Marianne gently to an awaiting Jeep, where Christine was already sitting.

"My apologies for the traveling accommodations, Marianne, but we couldn't risk any problems with you making a ruckus now could we?" Joshua said.

"Where are we going?" Marianne asked. "Where are we?"

Joshua smiled. "Welcome to Timmins, Ontario. And I am delivering you to an old friend."

"Delivering her?" Christine said.

"Yes," Joshua replied as the Jeep started up, then drove away.

"You see, I promised a very powerful magus here that 1 would deliver to him by the end of the year, a sacrifice for his Winter Solstice and since it is nearing 1 thought I should repay my debt."

Marianne sat in shock. She thought about jumping out of the jeep but that was silly, it was moving too fast. They were racing down the snow covered road. She looked at Christine, who just reached over and took Marianne's hand in hers and squeezed reassuringly.

When they reached a spot just outside of Timmins, they pulled into a large driveway which led up a hill to a large house. A neat looking man stood waiting for them and offered his hand to Marianne as she stepped out of the Jeep. She refused and got out on the other side with Christine.

"She will have to learn manners," the man said to Joshua.

"She will," Joshua replied.

Marianne decided to stay quiet. She thought, to reply would just give them too much satisfaction and she didn't want that. Not at all.

Marianne and Christine were led to a large room in the house with two beds and large sunlit windows that overlooked rolling hills of white.

"Gerald will see you shortly," the thin man said. "I am Rondel, 1 will see to your needs." Then he shut the door. Marianne ran to the closed door and listened carefully.

"You are no longer needed, Joshua," Rondel said. "The driver will return you to the airport."

"I will like to deliver her personally," Joshua replied.

"Gerald is not pleased with you, Joshua. He was expecting your gift a month ago so he could prepare her properly, you are lucky he is willing to take this now," Rondel said coldly. "The driver will return you to the airport."

Then Marianne heard footsteps walking away.

Not long after, Rondel opened the door again and announced he had come to bring Marianne to Gerald.

"You will not be needed yet," he said coldly to Christine, when she tried to follow.

"Why?" Christine asked.

Rondel closed and locked the door.

Marianne was led to a large sitting room. It was dark and dimly lit with candles. An alter was the prominent fixture in the room and pillows were scattered on the floor. Lying among one area of pillows was a slightly overweight dark skinned man of about forty.

"Come, sit," he said with a thick Jamaican accent. Marianne stood defiantly.

"I was informed you would be uncooperative," the man said. "I am Gerald Salem. You may stand, if you wish."

Marianne remained standing, aware that Rondel was behind her and to her left.

Gerald reached back and picked up a ripe apple from a dish behind him and bit into it. Marianne was suddenly aware of how hungry she was.

"You must be hungry," Gerald said. "If you wish to eat, come and sit."

Marianne remained standing, and said nothing.

"Very well." Gerald bit into the apple again and sat quietly eating, while Marianne stood in front of him. When he was done he stood and went before her.

"They tell me you are a Christian," he said. "Is this true?"

Marianne said nothing.

Gerald smiled wickedly at her and nodded at Rondel. Suddenly Marianne's legs erupted in a flurry of pain as Rondel brought a bamboo stick hard against the back of her thighs. Marianne fell to the floor and tears streaked her face as the sting from the blow dulled to a burning sensation.

Gerald reached down and jerked her face up to face his. "Remember this," he said. "I am master here. I control whether you live in comfort, or whether you live in pain. Do you understand?"

Marianne stared hard into Gerald's eyes, and said, "Jesus will save me."

Gerald smiled wider at Marianne. "Your Jesus doesn't care." With a nod from Gerald, another blow came down across Marianne's back, and she fell down on her stomach, more tears filling her eyes.

"Do you understand?" Marianne heard through the pain. "Your Jesus has no authority here! Only I do!"

She said nothing.

Another blow struck her in the side of the head, and then another, and another, until they melded together like a strange orchestration of pain. The last thing Marianne heard before she lost consciousness was Gerald's voice. "Take her to the Pit."

Jamie circled the airfield where Joshua landed. After a few moments, he brought The Skyhawk down and taxied it to a spot near where Joshua was overseeing the removal of the boxes.

"Let's go get them!" David screamed as he started to the door. Ben reached back and grabbed his friend by the shoulder and pulled him up to the cockpit window.

"See those," he said pointing to the lines of people standing by the boxes. "They'll rip us to shreds by the time we get close enough to touch the boxes. We have to be patient."

Jamie nodded and went to the back door. "Follow me," he said with a smile.

Ben looked at the others and shrugged his shoulders. They climbed out of the plane and ran around to one of the hangers that dotted the small airport. Holding their coats close to themselves they watched from their spot as the boxes were opened and the girls were loaded onto a jeep and driven away.

"What now, fearless leader?" Jamie asked as he looked to Ben. Ben watched as the Jeep drove away. Then he turned to Jamie.

"We catch a cab." He ran out into the road and stopped a passing cab, the door sign read, 'Daisy's Cab.'

The four young men crammed themselves into the small cab and Ben said, "Follow that Jeep!"

The man behind the wheel turned and said, with a thick Texan accent, "What'd he do, steal your girl?" Then he slammed on the gas and the cab raced away.

"Something like that," David replied.

The cab followed Joshua all the way to the house on the hill, then they had the driver stop just short of the driveway up the hill.

"Why don't we go up and get your little girl?" the Texan asked.

"It's a really delicate matter," Jamie said as he looked at the house.

The Texan nodded. "I get it, it's a government thing, and you guys can't talk about it. That's okay, I won't say a word."

Ben, David, Jamie and Steve all looked at each other in mild amusement.

"Why don't you take us to a car rental lot?" Ben said.

The Texan nodded and turned the car around, racing down the snow-covered road.

The small group split up, Steve and David went to City Hall to find out who owned the property on the hill and Ben and Jamie went to get the car. When they met again at a small restaurant, David noticed the car Ben and Jamie pulled up in and grimaced.

"Steve," David said. "You have to look at this."

Steve glanced out and saw Ben and Jamie stepping out of a dark green two door compact Volvo. "What?" he said. "How are we all going to fit into that thing?"

David shook his head in wonder.

Ben stepped up to the table, followed by Jamie and sat down smiling. He looked out at the car and waved an arm at it.

"What do you think?" he said with a big grin.

"How are we all going to fit in there?" Steve asked standing to his full 6'4". "We'll have to cut a hole for my head." He sat down again, flopping into his chair with a grunt.

"We're on a budget, I'm sorry," Jamie said. "But, we're driving the safest car in the world," he added with a smile.

David shook his head sorrowfully and pulled out his small notebook. "We got the name of the man who owns the house on the hill," he said. David paused as the waiter took their orders then continued as he walked away. "The name of the man is Gerald Salem. He's apparently independently wealthy and quite fond of giving money to the Town for rebuilding parks and such.

Ben nodded and looked out the window at the darkening sky. His hopes dropped at any attempt to get the girls today, he noticed the clouds were going to block the light of the moon.

"We'll have to get the girls tomorrow," he said. "It's just going to be too dark out tonight. He picked his home well."

Jamie nodded. "Yep, away from the town and all her nice bright lights."

David felt his heart fall as he looked out into the cold, darkening night of Northern Ontario.

When Martin and Mike got back to the house they found dinner ready and waiting for them. They sat down and ate what Collette and Sara had excellently prepared for them, sizzling hot steaks, prepared to perfection, and the baked potatoes steamed as the foil was removed.

At about six o'clock, there was a knock at the large oak door. Jeff answered it and found the black clad form of Raven standing at the door in a long trench coat. Jeff turned, and called back into the house, "Martin, Mike, I think there's someone here for you." Then he turned back to Raven. "Please come in."

Raven followed Jeff to the library, where the small group had previously decided to make their headquarters. Raven sat in the large plush couch and waited for the big police officer to arrive. When Martin walked into the room, Raven stood and extended his hand. Martin looked at it, then grasped it firmly.

"Good afternoon, Mister ... " Martin began.

"Raven, just Raven is fine, Detective," he replied.

"Just call me Martin."

Martin sat, and gestured towards the chair beside him. Raven sat and looked around the room calmly.

"Well," Martin said. "You wanted to talk to me."

Raven smiled and leaned forward. "You didn't get anything you wanted from Robert, I assume," he said.

"No, we didn't as a matter of fact," Martin replied. "You said you could help us."

Raven smiled. "Yes, I can."

"Will you?"

"Yes, I will." Raven leaned back and crossed his legs. "The man you're looking for is really Kriston Leigh."

Martin pulled out his notepad and pen from his shirt pocket.

"The other name he uses is Robert Darkfall," Raven said as he peered deeply into Martin's eyes.

Martin stopped writing, and stared at Raven intently.

"How do you know this?" Martin asked.

"I know that Robert was in Windsor on the days of the two murders," Raven explained. "I also know that on the nights of the two murders he came to my house and ordered me to dispose of his blood soaked clothes." Raven smiled viciously.

Martin's face lit up at Raven's statement. "So do you still have the clothes?"

Raven steepled his fingers in front of his face and smiled. "They are now in a safe in my basement."

"Will you testify to everything you've told me in a court?" Martin asked as he quickly wrote on his pad.

Raven shook his head, "No, you will have to get him through evidence, not testimony."

"Why help me then?"

"Because it helps me."

"How?"

"Because 1 am, and always will be Gideon's friend. No matter what name he goes by. The man is the same." Raven stood and walked

to the door of the library.

"Ben is different now, than when you knew him," Mike said. Raven stopped and slowly turned to face Mike. "Maybe, but he is, and always will be my friend. That will never change."

"If you give me your address I'll have some men pick up the bags ... " Martin started.

Raven shook his head. "No. I will have them sent to Ben's house."

Then he turned and opened the door. "I will see myself out, thank you."

Martin sat in the library for a long time after Raven left. There were so many unanswered questions still. How did Joshua Smith and Marianne fit into the plot? Why was Raven helping him? And the most pressing question was, what if he were walking into a trap?

Martin had to remember that he had civilians helping him in this case, because his superiors (obviously at the request of Robert or Joshua) had closed the case. What if one of them were injured in some way. He had already lost control of Marianne and the group that had gone after the girls, wherever they may be now. What if one of them were seriously injured, or even killed! How would he feel then? Or what if one of the students that were with him now were put in danger? What then?

Martin closed his eyes and silently asked God for help, not really expecting any. Then he pulled his tired bones out of the comfortable chair and walked up to his room, where he retired early from the day.

The next morning was bright, and a cool wind had cast a frost on everything it touched. Martin and the now smaller group of Sara, Mike and Collette were driven to the railway station by Collette's husband, Jeff.

Jeff wrapped his huge frame around Collette with a warm hug and a long kiss.

"I'll miss you. Be careful," he said, holding back tears.

"I will," Collette said as she brushed a tear that had fallen down his cheek. "Martin will keep us safe."

Martin wondered. Was he really able to do all that.

When Raven returned to Robert's house after seeing Martin he stepped out of the cab and found a young man in his twenties sitting on the porch waiting for him.

"Good evening, Charles," Raven said as he approached the house.

"Is there a problem?"

Charles stood and met Raven on the walkway. "There might be, Raven," he said in hushed tones. "Robert found out somehow, that you went to meet the detective."

Raven thought for a moment. "I knew that he would, Charles," he said.

Then he furrowed his brow. "But 1 did not think he would find out so quickly."

"I've gathered all the men who trust you, they are at Roland's house, waiting for you," Charles said. "Robert wants blood."

"Robert bathes in blood," Raven said calmly. "Take me to Roland's."

Charles led Raven to his car, and drove him to a small two story house Charles identified as Roland's. The house was painted white and sported an aluminum awning over the stained wood front porch. They climbed the stairs to the house and entered.

The first thing they saw was the blood. Then the stench of burnt flesh assaulted their senses. Charles ran out of the house and vomited over the railing of the porch, but Raven stood and took in all that he saw.

The bodies were lying on the floor in crumpled heaps, they seemed to have been ripped apart by some vicious creature that escaped from Raven's imagination. He couldn't even guess at how many bodies there were. Blood coated the walls and the furniture, as if they were painted.

Raven stepped over some of the corpses, walked into the kitchen, and down to the basement. Blood was everywhere. Raven scanned the massacre from the stairs and set all of what he saw to his memory.

To build my hate, he thought. To avenge your deaths.

When he was finished, he went back to the front door and saw something on the wall, just behind a couch. He walked over and pulled the couch away, careful not to leave fingerprints. What he saw broke his heart, and tears welled in his eyes. A child of about five was ripped to pieces and left behind the couch. Raven couldn't even tell its sex. It's small, bloody hand print was on the wall, just over its body.

Raven turned and walked out of the house, his eyes burning. Fifteen bodies, Raven thought, I think there were fifteen bodies. Charles was waiting in the car.

"We can't take you to the train station, Robert will expect that," Charles said when Raven got inside.

"Then take me home," Raven said.

"Yes, Superior," Charles said with a smile.

Raven looked at him, oddly for a moment and then smiled back weakly, forcing a leader's smile. He looked forward and vowed in his heart to avenge the blood of his people. Those people had trusted him to keep them safe from the war that was beginning between Raven and Robert, but Raven had failed to do that. Now they were dead ... forever.

# Chapter Twelve

The next morning, Ben stopped the car at the bottom of the hill, it was about two hundred meters away from the large house at the top of the hill. He got out, and studied the area around them. The trees, the hill and the shape of the hill.

To enter from the back would be impossible, Ben thought. The veranda goes out a good ten meters over the hill. The sides would be a better option. Even though there were no trees to block our advance.

David got out and stood behind Ben, watching him.

"Why did we stop?" he asked Ben, as he placed a hand on Ben's shoulder.

"I'm trying to figure out how we're going to get in," Ben said.

"Why don't we knock?" Steve said from the car.

Jamie pulled himself out through the window and sat on the door of the small car they rented the day before.

"And what would you like us to say?" he asked Steve. "Excuse me, sir, we're here to retrieve the girls you kidnapped. Can we have them please?"

Ben smiled and sat on the hood of the car, pulling his gloves tighter onto his hands. "He's got a point guys," he said to David and Steve.

"Well, let's try that before we go breaking into the guy's place," David said.

Ben sighed, and slid off the car, staring at the house.

"All right," he said finally. "We'll do it your way, David. But I do the talking, and we leave the car here."

Jamie pulled himself out of the car and went to where Ben was standing.

"You'll actually go up to this guy and talk to him about getting the girls back?" he yelled. "Salem'll just shoot you!"

"Jamie," Steve said as he got out of the car. "You've got to do something about that pessimism."

"Well, you can count me out," Jamie said. "Flying planes, yeah. Landings planes while trying not to let other planes see, sure. But walking into a death trap, no."

"Good," Ben said.

Jamie was surprised and stared at Ben oddly for a moment before asking, "Good?"

"Yeah, good," Ben replied. "We'll need someone here to drive us away when we get the girls out."

Jamie climbed back into the car and sat in the driver's seat. He pulled the seat up and eased into the vinyl.

"Fly, yes. Land, yes. Drive, yes," Jamie said with a crooked smile. "I like this job."

Ben smiled and led David and Steve towards the large house on the hill.

"What are you going to say?" Steve asked.

"I don't know," Ben answered.

"Are you going to ask for Gerald Salem?" David asked.

"I don't know," Ben replied.

"Uh, Ben, what are you going to do?" David said.

"I don't know," Ben smiled back at his friend.

David raised his eyebrows at Steve. "Talk about following the Lord," he said.

Marianne woke, lying on a pile of frozen straw. She was now wearing a rough cloth dress, she had nothing else on and a dirty wool blanket had been thrown over her. She had been stripped and dressed while she was unconscious and now she felt violated. She felt the growing welt on the side of her face and winced as the touch brought a shock of pain up her temple.

She tried to stand, and found it difficult with the welts and bruises on the backs of her legs as well. The cold made it hard to stand and move around.

As Marianne looked around she saw the room she was in was really more of a dug out hole than a room. The walls were dirt and the floor was dirt, covered with rotting frozen straw. There were no windows in her prison, but a little light came through the wooden cover that closed the top of the pit.

It didn't take long, but Marianne found if she reached up and stood on her toes she could touch the cover, but it was too heavy for her to lift, or move. After that, she fell to the ground, sobbing for Jesus to come and save her, as she pulled the wool blanket close, hoping for warmth.

Christine was left in the room, after Marianne was taken. She sat on the large bed, until Rondel came back carrying a large tray of food. Christine suddenly realized how hungry she was.

"Good evening," Rondel said. "I trust the accommodations are adequate?"

Christine eyed the man with care. "Yes, they are," she said, choosing her words carefully. "Where is Marianne?"

Rondel set the tray on a table a few feet from the bed and pulled a chair out, motioning for Christine to sit in it.

"She has gone away with Gerald for awhile," he said as Christine sat in the chair. "She most likely won't be back for a long time."

Christine said a quiet grace and then looked up at Rondel.

"Where did they go?" she asked as she cut a piece of meat.

"I do not know." Rondel pulled a second chair up to the table.

"There are some things that we have to discuss."

Christine looked up from her food. "Like what?" she asked after she had swallowed.

"Like your rules."

Christine cocked her head, as she generally did when she was confused.

"You are not allowed to leave your room," Rondel continued. "At least not now. If you prove cooperative I will take you outside twice a day, if you wish."

"What about the bathroom?" Christine asked with a smile.

"Behind that door," Rondel pointed at a door behind him, "is a private bath for you."

Rondel stood and walked towards the door to the hall. "Next week, perhaps, you will be allowed to walk the house freely," he said. "But not now. Enjoy your meal, I will return to gather the dishes."

When the door closed, Christine sat in silence and stared at her food for a moment. Then she stood and walked to her bed, fell and wept into her pillow, until she fell asleep.

The next morning she found her breakfast set on the table and her dishes from the night before removed. There was also a change of clothes laid across the chair for her.

They were expensive clothes and would have cost a fortune. But, there they were, in her size and newly pressed. She stood and went to the bath, where she found fresh towels and unopened bars of soap and shampoo.

She bathed and wrapped herself in a large, plush, flannel house coat and went to eat her breakfast.

After she finished her meal of bacon and scrambled eggs, she dressed in the clothes provided and sat on a large, leather couch.

She noticed a bookcase on the far wall, and as she went to investigate it she noticed a copy of the Holy Bible. She took it down and returned to the couch, opening the Bible to the Book of Psalms. This should help me cope, she thought.

After she read through the first two chapters there was a knock on the door.

"Come in?" She called, curious that anyone would knock for a prisoner.

The door opened and a small, heavy-set dark skinned woman walked into the room. Christine placed the Bible on the couch beside her, and stood to greet the new face.

"Hello," the woman said.

"Hi," Christine smiled. "You're a new face."

The woman walked over to the table and picked up the dirty dishes.

"My name is Joanna. I'll be cleaning your room and seeing if you need anything," Joanna said in a thick Jamaican accent. She glanced at the couch and saw the Bible sitting beside Christine.

"You better not let Rondel see that Bible, Miss." Joanna pointed at the book. "He be very angry if he finds out I left that here for you." She smiled and winked at the girl on the couch. "There were rumors going around the house you were a Christian, so I took a chance and brought one of my Bibles over for you ... just in case they were true."

Christine smiled warmly at the pudgy Jamaican. "Joanna, you're an answer to prayer."

Martin, Sara, Mike and Collette climbed off the train and collected their baggage. Mike had packed his roommates' belongings for them, there was no time to think about packing for the sudden trip.

The train ride was quiet for everyone. The tension and the worry the small group was feeling over the sudden absence of David, Marianne, Christine and Ben was immense. The two men had been the focal point for the entire investigation, and now they were gone, there seemed to be a huge hole in the bond they felt. The kidnapping of Marianne and Christine only intensified the need to find the true killer, and put him in jail.

Martin told them what Raven said about Robert. At first they were very excited about the prospect of having the proof to finish the case. Then Martin reminded them Joshua Smith was involved too and they had to find a link to him.

"If Ben and David get the girls back we'll be able to put him away for kidnapping," Martin said. He looked at the group's shocked faces for a moment before he realized what was wrong. "I mean, when they bring her back," he added sheepishly.

Martin hailed a cab and threw his bags in the trunk, then helped the others with their bags.

"440 California street," Martin told the cab driver.

Sara looked back at the small gray car David drove. It was still in the train parking lot, gathering snow as it sat unused.

"David's going to pay a bunch for parking," she said, trying to make conversation.

"Yeah, it's going to add up after awhile," Mike added.

They rode the rest of the way in silence.

When the small group of four got into the house on California, Mike put his stuff into his room and showed Collette to David's room, where she would sleep.

"I'd like to stay in Ben's room," Sara said. "If that's okay with you."

"Sure," Mike smiled, glad that he wouldn't be alone. "That would be great."

Martin sat in the high-backed chair beside the fireplace, absently tossing logs into it.

"Alright guys," he said in a business-like fashion. "We have to talk about what comes next."

"Well," Mike said as he sat on the couch. "You're the detective, why don't you tell us?"

Sara smiled and sat beside Mike. "Well, we could go back to the library and find out the names of the other pastors who were involved in the debate."

"Yeah," Martin said. "That would be the next course of action."

"We'll do that tomorrow?" Collette said, from her chair by the large picture window.

"Yeah," Martin said as he stretched. "Let's take tonight off."

"Good!" Collette said as she stood and rolled her sleeves up.

"Now we can see what kind of food there is in this house."

Charles and Raven drove through the night to get to Windsor. The four hour drive gave Raven a great deal of time to think about his next course of action. He was willing, if he had to, to kill Robert, but he hoped it wouldn't come to that.

Raven wondered what Ben would think if he knew that Raven was willing to kill the friend that Robert once was to both of them. No, not Robert. Robert Darkfall was never a friend to either Ben or Raven. Kriston Liegh was the friend to them.

Something had happened.. Kriston went on a trip to Toronto, it lasted two years. At first he was writing, and then the letters stopped. All three had been a part of the same cult, and Raven and Gideon wondered if they would see Kriston at one of the yearly conventions the cult held.

The first convention came and went and neither Gideon nor Raven saw Kriston. Then, during the next year, Gideon was saved, and became Ben again, and at the next convention, Raven met the new Superior of the cult of

Ctchutic, Robert Darkfall.

Kriston had become cold and hard. He had given up his name, a thing he said he'd never do. Raven and Ben had taken on different names, but Kriston said it would make him feel like he was giving up his identity.

Maybe he had.

Charles pulled into Raven's driveway and turned off the car. Raven stopped him, when Charles started out of the car.

"Wait here," Raven said as he stared at his house.

Raven stepped out of the car and pulled his black trench coat tight around his lean frame. The stairs up the porch creaked slightly as Raven climbed, and the lock seemed impossibly loud as he turned it.

Raven stepped into the house and noticed a blur to his side. He jumped onto his couch and pulled a knife that was sheathed on his hip. The body jumped at Raven with a blunt object raised in his hand, causing Raven to turn and fall off his couch and onto the floor. Raven pushed himself up and drove the knife down and into the body on the couch. A short scream cut the air, a bloody gurgle, and then silence.

A few moments later Charles rushed into the house, holding a gun.

"Raven?" he said softly.

"Down here," Raven said from where he sat beside the non-moving form. "Call Robertson at the Police Department, he's one of ours."

Charles went to the phone, dialed the number, and asked for Chief Robertson.

"Yes, we have a problem with an intruder here," Charles said into the phone. "He's dead."

There was silence for a moment, then Charles hung the phone up.

"He says he'll be here in a few minutes to take care of it." Charles went to the kitchen. "Would you like me to make you a tea?" he asked nonchalantly.

Raven turned to Charles, a strange look in his eyes. Was death that simple now? "Yes, please," he said, trying to hide the growing horror at what he was becoming. He reached up and switched the light on. He immediately recognized the face. "It's Frank," he said. "One of Robert's gunmen. The same man that went with me to take care of Damien."

"So Robert's behind this?" Charles called from the kitchen.

"Who else?" Raven said dryly. Raven stood and walked to the stairs leading to his basement. Charles came with a cup of hot tea and offered it to Raven.

"In a moment," Raven said distractedly. "I have to check something."

Raven went downstairs to the room where Ben found the books so many days before. He went to a side wall, and pushed on a hidden trigger mechanism and part of the wall clicked and swung open, revealing a safe with a tumbler lock.

Raven quickly dialed the combination and pulled the safe door open. There sitting in the safe amidst various old books and papers was a large garbage bag.

Raven sighed in relief, and pulled the bag out of the safe opening it. Inside was the pile of bloody clothes. He smiled and closed the bag, and carried it upstairs.

When Raven emerged from the stairs, Charles looked at the bag, and frowned curiously. Raven smiled in response and placed the bag on the floor.

"Open it," Raven commanded.

Charles paused for a moment at Raven's commanding tone, and then handed Raven his tea, which he sipped contentedly. Then Charles tentatively opened the bag, his eyes widened and he closed it again.

"What...?" Charles started.

"Robert's clothes, Charles," Raven said with an evil smile.

"Robert has a weakness, and this is it."

Ben, David and Steve walked up to the large house and Ben knocked on the door. A few moments later the door opened and Rondel stood in front of them in a Grey silk suit.

"Can I help you?" he asked.

Ben thought for a moment, looking Rondel in the eyes. "Yes. We're here looking for a girl named Marianne Storm," Ben said calmly.

Rondel's eyes narrowed for a moment and then he smiled. "I'm sorry, I don't know of anyone by that name."

"I think you do," Ben replied without a pause. "We know that Joshua Smith, brought her here and turned her over to your boss, Gerald Salem."

Rondel's face went blank. "Your information is faulty, sir." Rondel went to close the door.

"I don't think you would want to close the door," Ben said as he jammed his foot in the doorway. "Unless you want an investigator from the RCMP knocking on it next."

Suddenly, a hand rested on Rondel's shoulder just as he was about to respond. A handsome Jamaican face peered over Rondel's shoulder.

"You should not be so rude to guests to our house, Rondel," the face said. "Come in. Be welcome in the house of Gerald Salem." Gerald stepped out of the way and held the door open for Ben and his friends to walk in.

Ben thanked Gerald for his courtesy and led the others into the warm house.

"How can we help you?" Gerald said confidently. He stopped suddenly, and threw up his hands. "I forget my manners. Can I get you something warm to drink? You look like you've seen much travel and the air outside is very cold today."

Ben looked down at his clothes and chuckled a bit. They didn't have time to pack before they left, nor to stop to buy new clothes, they were crumpled and dirty. "Yes, perhaps some coffee, please," Ben replied.

David and Steve both nodded their heads in agreement, not saying a word.

Gerald motioned to a thin woman who went into the hall and disappeared. A few moments later she came back with a tray. On the tray was a coffee pot and four mugs.

"Come into the parlor, please," Gerald said with a smile.

"Said the spider to the fly," Steve muttered under his breath. Gerald led them into a lavishly decorated sitting room. He sat in a leather recliner and poured coffee for the three young men, handing each of them a mug.

"The reason we're here ... " Ben began.

"Is to find you're friend, Marianne Storm. Correct?" Gerald finished.

Ben smiled and nodded his head. "There's a second girl too, Christine Scott." He sipped at the coffee and frowned at the odd taste. He glanced over at David and Steve and saw that their mugs were already half empty. Ben stood and felt the room spin.

"What?" he said as he stepped up towards Gerald.

Rondel walked in behind Gerald and caught David as he slipped out of his chair and onto the floor. Then he eased Steve out of his chair as he, too fell unconscious.

Ben turned and fell. He felt his fall interrupted by a pair of strong hands, that eased him to the floor and he heard Rondel's voice, "You should have let her go."

# Chapter Thirteen

Marianne had been trapped in the pit for a long time. The minutes dragged into hours and the hours dragged on and on. She had no idea how long she had been there. Only that it seemed an eternity.

No food had been dropped down to her and her stomach was beginning to cry and growl from hunger pangs. At times, she tried to claw her way up to push the lid off the hole but she couldn't get the leverage she needed. She was starting to lose feeling in her arms and legs and her shivering was becoming uncontrollable.

Finally, the lid was suddenly removed and Rondel lowered a rope to her.

"Tie this around your waist," he ordered.

"What are you going to do after that?" Marianne asked as she held the rope in her hand.

"If you want food and warmth, you will tie the rope around your waist," Rondel replied.

Marianne quickly tied the rope, her need for warmth and food greater than her pride, Rondel hoisted her out of the pit. She could see now, it was night and the stars cast a dull glow on the landscape all around her. Gerald's house was here, Rondel led her to the back door of the house and into one of the bathrooms.

"You'll find clothes in there," he said as he untied the rope and rolled it up again. "Change, and clean up before dinner."

After Marianne went into the room, she heard the door being locked, and Rondel walk away. She quickly looked around the room for something she could use as a weapon. All she found was a bar of soap, a bottle of shampoo, a washcloth and a towel.

"Nothing useful in here," she said to herself.

She sat on the toilet and regarded herself in the mirror on the wall.

She was dirty and disheveled, her hair was matted, almost brown from dirt, and her face was covered with scratches and dried blood.

Marianne put her face in her hands and cried. She cried long and hard, until finally, there were no more tears left in the world to keep her crying. Then she lifted her head, and with a short prayer for strength from the Lord she went into the shower turned the water very warm, and cleaned herself.

Rondel returned to the bathroom and unlocked it. Marianne emerged a moment later in a long, black evening dress with various co loured sequins.

"You look very lovely," Rondel said. "This way to dinner." Rondel led Marianne through the large house, and into a big dinning room where Gerald was sitting in a large chair at the head of the table. Large graceful curves gilded the comers of the room. Marianne gasped as she saw intricate carvings of daemons and dark, onyx gargoyles. The table was ten feet long and took up the majority of the centre of the large room. There were two settings, one for Gerald at the head of the dark table and another to his left.

"Good evening, dear. I trust you are more talkative now?" Gerald said, as he stood and took Marianne's hand in his. Marianne shivered as a cold chill ran up her spine.

Marianne nodded. "Yes, I am, as long as I enjoy the conversation." Gerald smiled and guided her to her chair and eased it back as Marianne sat. Rondel walked up behind her and stood off to her left where she couldn't see him.

"What's going to happen to me?" Marianne asked, not really wantmg an answer.

"That all depends on how you react to what happens to you," Gerald said in an evasive manner.

A tall thin man dressed in a white servers uniform walked into the room carrying a tray. He set the tray on a table and placed a bowl of steaming soup in front of Gerald, then returned with another for Marianne.

Marianne silently thanked the Lord for the food and asked that He purify it for her and joined Gerald.

"I believe in a few days you may be allowed to accompany me to an island I own, just off the coast of Jamaica," Gerald said in an easy manner.

"And what would you do there?" Marianne asked, fear building in the pit of her stomach.

"I do a great many things on that island," Gerald said with a blank face; she couldn't read him. Yet there was something in the set of his eyes that said she wouldn't want to know what he did anyway.

"Do you like to swim?" Gerald asked.

"Yes. Why?" Marianne replied wondering what would come next.

"There is a large private lagoon on my island," Gerald said. "I believe you would like to swim there if given the chance." Then his eyes hardened and Marianne stopped the spoon halfway to her mouth.

"But you must learn to be cooperative."

Marianne lowered the spoon back to the bowl. "And what constitutes 'cooperative'?"

"You must obey when spoken to, listen to what I say, and take it as the law."

"I only go by the law laid out in the Bible," Marianne said defiantly. Her head suddenly jerked to the side as Rondel's hand lashed out and hit her in the back of the head.

"Simply because I gave you good clothes to wear does not mean you will not be punished." Gerald smiled as he lifted the warm soup to his lips.

"Did you know we had some visitors here?"

Marianne stared at Gerald with a sick expression. Who could they be? she thought. He said it as if she should know who they were. Who would come to look for her?

"Who is it?" she asked with her stomach in her throat. "Who are the visitors?"

Gerald smiled and pulled out three wallets, throwing them at her.

"See for yourself," he said.

Marianne opened each and saw Ben's, David's and Steve's identification. What was Steve doing here? She put the wallets in a neat pile beside her plate, struggling to put the panic behind her. "How are they?" she asked, her voice shook only once.

"Dead," Rondel said from behind her. "I cut their bellies open and made them watch as I scooped out their entrails."

Marianne's face fell and she spun around to slap Rondel but her hand was caught by his iron strong grip. "Let go!" She screamed.

"So you can slap me?" Rondel replied. "I think not."

Marianne shot her eyes towards Gerald, who was calmly finishing his soup. The thin man walked back in and removed the soup bowls, replacing them with plates of a green salad. He left quietly. Marianne pulled her hand, but Rondel held it fast. Her eyes were beginning to well up with tears.

"They screamed well," Rondel continued. "Too bad you were in the Pit. You could have heard them." He reached over and seized her face with his free hand, locking her eyes with his. "They were strong boys, they lived long and they died slowly, even after they lost consciousness."

Rondel released her hand and her chin, then took a step back to where he had been standing. Marianne swung back in her seat, and stared hard at Gerald. "Was that your order?" she asked through the tears.

Gerald looked up at her and smiled. "Yes, my dear, and if you do not behave as you are expected, I will ensure that more of your precious friends are disposed of in ways that will not be as ... gentle."

Ben woke up lying on his side in a dark room. As he sat up, and waited for his eyes to adjust to the lack of light, he heard some whispering not far from him.

"David? Steve?" Ben said softly.

"Ben? Good, you're up. Do you have any idea where we are?"

David's voice replied.

"No." Ben could see the vague outlines of his friends now. He could also see the heavy wood door which held them in the dark room.

"How could I? The last thing I remember is drinking the worst tasting coffee in the world."

Ben stood and fought off a sudden attack of dizziness.

"Easy, Ben it takes a while to reorient yourself," Steve said.

Ben nodded, and stumbled to the door. A thin wash of light seeped from the crack at the bottom of the door, Ben saw there was no carpet on the other side, as he peeked under the door.

"Well, we're not in the same house," Ben said. "There isn't a carpet on the other side of the door."

"Hey, that's great," Steve said sarcastically. "Now all we have to do is get out of this room and we'll be just as lost as we are here."

Ben studied the door a bit longer. "Do you really want to get out?" he asked.

"Well, I sure don't want to stay here," Steve replied.

Ben knocked on the door. When no response came Steve laughed at him.

"Did you think they'd just let you out?" he said with a smile.

"No," Ben replied, smiling as well. He spun on his left foot and whipped his right foot around, performing a spinning kick that knocked the door off its hinges and smashed it into the far wall. "Got to learn tact!" he said with a grin.

"Time to check out of this hotel!" David said as he got up and ran towards the hall.

The hall ran to the left and the right. Down the left passage was a door and to the right, and they saw the hall curved to the left again.

David chose the left passage. "This looks like as good a way as any," he said to the others.

"If I were a kidnapper where would I keep the hostages?" Steve said softly.

Ben smiled. "In the tower?"

"That's only if we were in 'Merry Old England,'" David said over his shoulder with a fake accent.

When David reached the door at the end of the hall, he stopped and put his ear against it.

"Is the door telling you anything?" Steve said.

David looked up at the tall young man. "I was listening to see if anyone was on the other side."

"And?" Steve replied.

"I hear some chanting, in a low voice. And there's some drums and what sounds like a ... chicken?" David frowned in confusion.

"Their singing to a chicken?" Steve smiled.

Ben rushed forward and put his ear to the door. His face wrinkled in concentration for a moment and then he recited what he heard, "Tarry, pimpkin, in this tree, till such time as full ye be." Ben stepped back and looked at his two companions. "They're not singing to the chicken, their about to sacrifice it to the daemon, Cagrino."

"How do you know all that?" Steve asked.

Ben smiled. "Wasted youth."

Ben started back up the way they came, quickly followed by the two other young men. "Cagrino is a daemon that was mainly worshiped by gypsies." Ben looked back and smiled at David and Steve.

"That's why gypsies have such a bad reputation. Would you want to be friends with someone that worshiped something called Cagrino?"

Ben led them back the way they came and up the hall that curved left. The doors lining the hall were solid and made of a stout wood none of them recognized. David opened some of the doors, and reported the rooms were empty with the exception of a cot, some clothes and toiletries.

"Everyone's probably at the ceremony," Steve said softly. "That means we should be able to sneak out."

Ben nodded. "However, should and will are two different things.

For some stupid reason we thought we could just ask Gerald for the girls too."

"Momentary insanity," David muttered.

Steve opened the far door at the end of the hall and peered out. A stream of sunlight burst through and illuminated the hall, causing the three men to shield their eyes. Steve reported they were at a large building which resembled a school.

Steve led them across a dirt covered courtyard and into a blockedoff area where they found a large pasture of grazing goats and a few horses, saddled and roped off at a tree.

"Do you guys know how to ride?" David asked with a meaningful glance at the horses.

Steve and Ben exchanged unsure looks at each other and both said they could manage before easing towards the large muscled animals.

David smoothly leaped up onto the back of a large gray stallion and wheeled the animal around with sure hand and knee movements.

He smiled softly as he saw the other two sitting uneasily on top of their mounts.

"Have you guys ever ridden before?" David asked.

"No," Steve replied as he nearly fell off the restless animal.

David's amused smile was only half hidden.

"I've lived in a city all my life, David," Ben said. "I didn't get many chances to go riding a horse down main street."

After a few moments of direction from David the three young men lumbered up road towards the house that sat on the hill, far away. Ben and Steve were constantly complaining about the bumpy ride, and their uncertainty about staying on top of the big animals. They vowed the first chance they got, they should leave the beasts and rent another car.

"I rather like this mode of transportation," David replied with a wry smile. "It makes us seem more hero-like."

"Hero's can ride in Volvo's too," Ben said, shifting to a more comfortable position for the hundredth time.

After a little while David taught them to trot, and then to gallop, which was a greater pain as far as the other two were concerned. So, they continued on at a slow walk, never taking their eyes off the darkening snow covered road ahead.

"They probably know that we've broken out by now," Ben said as they crested a hill.

"What will we do if they come after us in cars?" Steve asked. "We should go into town and rent a car." He smiled at the comment.

"We could gallop into the fields," David said, grinning. Ben and Steve winced.

"What will we do when we get to the house again?" Steve asked after a short silence. Then he looked at David with a severe smile. "I am not going to gallop into the house on a horse."

David looked slightly upset at the prospect of not being able to ride horses into the house but he swung his leg over the pommel of the saddle and wondered what to do next.

"I think our best idea would be to go to the police," he said finally.

"1 can see it now," Ben said. "Excuse me but we have a problem.

Our friends have been kidnapped. Who kidnapped them? The nice man that gives your town all the money." Ben started laughing softly at the idea.

"What can we do that will work?" David asked in a strained voice.

His eyes were far away and he shook his head to look at Ben. "Well?"

Ben shook his head sadly, "I don't know."

Jamie was sitting on the hood of the rented car for quite some time before he started to get worried. A car had ripped out of the drive of the house and shot up the road in a hurry a few hours ago. He had considered following it, but he figured he should stay where he was until the other three came back. He looked up at the darkening sky and sighed deeply.

"O.K. Jamie," he said softly to himself. "Here you are, in the snow belt. Normally I would like that idea, I could go skiing, but I have to wait here for my friends, and save a couple of girls from the evil clutches of a major Occult leader. And to top it off, I'm talking to myself." Jamie closed his eyes and sighed heavily. "This is going to be a bad week."

He hopped off the car and walked to the edge of the road and stared at the house. The sun was setting and still no sign of Ben or the others. Jamie turned angrily and hopped back into the warmth of the car.

"I am not going in to save their butts," he said sternly to himself. "I am not going to risk my life any more than I have to."

He sat in the driver's seat for a few moments before he jumped out and went to the trunk of the small car. Inside he found a few flares and a length of rope. Just what he needed. He stuffed the flares and the rope into a gym bag and started to trudge up the hill, away from the road.

"Alright, so I lied," Jamie muttered. "Here I am going to break into the house of a major Occult leader, who's probably going to sacrifice me to some ugly daemon to save a bunch of idiots that don't know what their doing."

Jamie ran softly up to the house and rolled under one of the windows. The sky was slowly darkening, and the air was growing colder by the minute. The hair on Jamie's body was trying to stand on end under his clothes. He wasn't sure if it was the cold air, or the fear in his head.

He slowly crept to the back door and tried to turn the knob. It moved easily and smoothly, quietly clicking open. Jamie nodded his head in satisfaction and crept around to the other side of the house. There he took one of the flares out and counted the remains. Three left, plus the one in his hand. He lit the flare by pulling on the small string in the end, and threw it into an open window and into the front room.

The room inside burst into light and a few startled screams could be heard. Jamie paused for a satisfied smile and then ran around and to a window on the other side of the large mansion, tossing another flare through the window, with the same result. Twice more he lobbed the bright flares into the house and then ran to the rear, where he had found the open door.

Pulling the rope out of the bag, and leaving the bag on the back porch, Jamie rushed into the house and began his search for the girls, and the three missing men.

# Chapter Fourteen

Gerald jerked his head towards the sound of crashing glass.

"What was that?" he asked.

"We're being attacked!" Rondel yelled. Suddenly a flare crashed through one of the windows and ignited on the rug.

"Take the girl back to the Pit and meet me in my rooms," Gerald screamed in anger as he ran up the back stairs.

Rondel looked down at Marianne and smiled. "Come, girl, it's back to the Pit with you."

Marianne stood and tried to run, but Rondel reached out and grabbed her arm in a vice-like grip. He raised his other hand and brought it down on her face, splitting her lip.

"You will learn respect, girl," Rondel muttered as he pulled her out the back door, towards the old, dark hole.

When they reached the Pit, Rondel turned and struck Marianne on the chin with his fist. Marianne fell and knelt on the ground, disoriented. Rondel removed the wooden cover and kicked Marianne in the stomach, causing her to roll into a fetal position, coating the black dress in snow. Rondel muttered some curses and kicked her again and again until she fell into the Pit with a dull thud.

The cover was returned and Rondel walked back into the house, never even hearing the crying from the Pit.

The sun was almost completely gone when the three men on horseback rode over the crest of the hill and started down the other side and towards the small, green Volvo parked on the side of the road.

David pushed his horse, which he had named Yeshua, into a quick trot to get to the side of the car. Climbing down off of Yeshua he peered into the car as the others reached him.

"Jamie's not here!" David said, as he looked to the others, who were still sitting on their horses. Steve named his horse Moses, at David's urging, and Ben's was Job, more for the suffering the horse was causing him. Ben glanced up at the house on the hill, and frowned.

"What's that look like to you guys?" he said pointing up at the top of the hill. As the other two young men looked up at the hill they saw that the house was on fire. Flames licked at the siding through broken windows and people milled around in the snow outside the large mansion.

"Marianne," David whispered softly.

"No," Ben said dryly. "Jamie."

David wheeled himself onto the leather saddle and pushed him into a hard gallop up the hill towards the house. Grudgingly, Steve and Ben followed.

As they approached the building, they saw only anarchy. People were milling about with buckets and hoses, trying to put out the fires. Getting only a few startled stares, David led the other two around the back of the house towards the rear entrance. David leapt off Yeshua and burst into the burning building, with Ben and Steve close behind.

"David," Ben sputtered through the smoke. "How do you expect to find anybody?"

"I don't know," David said as he ran up the stairs.

"Sounds like the same plan we had before," Steve mumbled under his breath.

Ben nodded, "It didn't work then either."

David led the others into a large bed chamber, where they found Gerald standing over the cowering figure of Rondel, with a gun to his head.

"You were in charge of security I" he finished before turning on the three startled men. "You three! You did this! You are responsible for this!" He turned the gun on them.

Jamie turned the comer into another hallway. The smoke wasn't as bad in this area of the mansion and he had only run into a few servants who were milling about trying to save what belongings they could from the fire.

"This house is too big," Jamie said to himself. As he turned another comer, what seemed to be the hundredth, he ran full on into a short, plump dark-skinned woman carrying an armful of clothes.

"Who are you?" she asked with a heavy accent. "I've never seen you around here before."

Jamie helped the woman to her feet and then said, carefully, "I'm looking for two girls."

The woman studied his face for a moment then grabbed his hand and led him down the hall.

"My name is Joanna, I will bring you to one of them." She stopped in front of a door and fiddled with some keys. "The other is in the Pit," she added softly as she opened the door.

Jamie rushed in, followed by Joanna. Standing beside the bed with a blanket wrapped around her was Christine. She looked at Joanna and then noticed Jamie. Christine rushed to Jamie and gripped him in a huge hug that nearly choked him.

"How did you find us? Where are the others? Did you start the fire? Is Mike with you?" she asked quickly pushing him away. She obviously expected answers now.

"We followed you. I don't know. Yes. No," Jamie said as he pulled

Christine out the door. Joanna followed behind Christine. "Joanna, where's this 'Pit'?"

"Follow me," Joanna said trotting up the hall again. "I'll take you the back way."

"You're the only one that came?" Christine asked.

"Ben, Steve and David are here too," Jamie said. "They came into the house earlier this afternoon but I haven't seen them since."

"Well, where could they have gone?"

"1 don't know."

Then they heard the gunshots.

Ben jumped to the floor and rolled towards Gerald just as he fired the first shot. Out of the comer of his eye he saw Steve and David jumping to their sides. Thank God, he's a bad shot, Ben thought.

Rolling to his feet, he stumbled over the still cowering form of Rondel and missed getting shot by the second shot and the next two that came in rapid succession. He saw Rondel's head explode with the impact of one of the bullets and fall back onto the plush carpet.

"Die!" Gerald screamed. "Die, you fool!"

Ben struck out with his leg and caught Gerald in the knee sending the next bullet into the ceiling as he fell. David jumped onto Gerald and pinned his gun-hand onto the floor. As Ben stood again, Gerald punched David in the side of the head, knocking him down and rolling on the carpet. Gerald shot another round towards Ben, who grabbed his arm as the bullet nicked him. Gerald turned the gun on David and fired another shot that went wide as Steve careened into his side. Gerald spun Steve around and flung him onto the bed as easily as if he was a rag doll.

As David stood up, he saw the barrel of the gun leveled on him.

Ben walked up beside his friend holding his arm, which was sticky with blood. Steve climbed off the bed and stood behind them.

"Now," Gerald said, "Now I have you." Smoke was filtering in through the open door and the sound of the fire downstairs seemed like a roar that could only come from a daemon. Gerald's face was a mask of insane ecstasy as he leveled the gun on David's head. He slowly pulled the trigger and his face melted when he only heard a flat click.

Ben suddenly stepped forward and spun on one foot as he brought the other hard against Gerald's head sending him to the floor, unconscious.

"Looks like I'm not the only blessed one," Ben said as he turned to David.

"Praise God," David said weakly. "Thank you, Jesus!"

Steve quickly ripped a piece of sheet off the bed and bandaged Ben's arm. "We have to find the girls," he said as he tightened the knot on the makeshift bandage.

David led the way out the door and up the hall again. After a quick search of all the rooms on the second floor they stopped at the top of the stairs and stared down at the rapidly burning first floor. The stairs had collapsed and the fire was slowly crawling its way up.

Joshua opened the door to his house, and walked in. He dropped his bag onto the floor and sat in a large plush chair. He turned no lights on, preferring to sit and think in the dark about what he would do next, if the annoying students were to gather the nerve to knock on his door about the disappearance of Marianne and the other one.

Things were getting touchy now, and he had to handle them with very soft hands, and the only way to do that was to sit and think. Joshua believed he could figure anything in the world out if he just sat and thought about the problem.

His first thought was to break all ties with anyone who was involved in the killings. In order to sever those ties, however, he would have to kill those involved, and that would bring a great deal of interest into Occult activity in Toronto.

"I am glad to see you returned safely, Joshua," Robert's voice came from the dark recesses of the hall.

Joshua stood and faced the shadow. "What are you doing here? I didn't invite you."

Robert looked at the floor and shook his head. "That is none of my concern. Raven and you were the only people who knew I killed those clergy. Your little scheme may keep the university students away, however, the detective has a friend in higher places than I. I need your assurance, that whatever I say you will do."

"1 am not one of your thugs, Robert," Joshua said with a negligent flip of his hand and walked towards the sherry decanter on a small wooden table.

Robert pulled a knife out of his coat pocket. "I suppose you're not," he said, then he drove the knife deep into Joshua's back. "A foolish decision, on your part," he said over Joshua's dying body.

Martin woke the following morning to the sound of his wailing alarm clock. He got up, showered, dressed and ate his usual breakfast of two pieces of toast and a cup of very strong coffee.

Before he went to the office, he wanted to drop in and see Mike and the girls. He pulled into the driveway and noticed a large bag sitting on the front porch. He quickly got out and ran to the bag, his heart pounding. As he opened it he saw the clothes inside, covered in dried blood. He quickly closed the bag, shoved it in the back seat of his car, and locked it, then he went to the front door, knocked and walked in.

"Hello!" Martin called.

Mike walked down the stairs and smiled at Martin. "Hi how are you doing?" he asked.

"There was a bag on your front porch this morning. It's the clothes of whomever killed the clergy," Martin smiled.

Mike smiled broadly. "Then we've almost got him!"

Martin nodded. "Yes, all we have to do is make a blood match to prove that they were the clothes worn by the killer, and then do a skin sample to prove Robert Darkfall wore the clothes."

Mike went to the kitchen and made himself and Martin a cup of coffee. "The girls and I are going to go find out exactly who was at the debate that triggered the murders."

"That's a good idea," Martin said. "I'll have the Toronto Police pick up Robert Darkfall, or Kriston Leigh, whatever is his real name, and have him sent here for questioning."

Mike smiled, finished his coffee and saw Martin to the door, "To do you want to come over here tonight for Bible Study?"

Martin frowned, "I don't know, 1 mean with the case being almost over and everything 1 just thought we'd go back to our normal lives,"

Mike shook his head. "No, we'd like you to come to our studies.

You're our friend now and we still want you around." Mike clapped the big man on the shoulder. "Just because the case is over it doesn't mean that the friendship is."

"I'll see you tonight then, 6:00?" Martin smiled

"You bet!" Mike exclaimed.

Martin got in his car and drove to his office. Carrying the garbage bag into the precinct he went immediately to forensics, where he dropped off the bag and its contents, and saw that they were properly filed, and coded into the computer.

Then he went upstairs and wrote out an arrest warrant for Robert Darkfall and Kriston Leigh. After a short walk he dropped the forms off at the provincial courthouse and waited for a free judge.

At about 1 :30 p.m. he was called into the office of an older judge named John Senko. Martin smiled and glanced around the chambers, with the usual observant eyes of a detective. He first noticed a poster that was framed and hanging on the judge's far wall It read: "God grant me the serenity to accept the things 1 cannot change, the strength to change the things I can, and the wisdom to know the difference."

Martin smiled and looked at the judge.

"I noticed you looking at my prayer, there on the wall detective," the older man said as he closed a file folder. "It's something we can really learn from."

"Yes, sir," Martin replied politely.

Judge Senko leaned back and rubbed his eyes. "1 pray that every morning when 1 walk into these chambers, but 1 still make bad decisions sometimes. 1 guess God just wants us to make sure that we know we're still humans and still fallible."

Martin smiled and nodded his head. "That in itself is a very wise statement, sir."

Judge Senko nodded and then looked down at the papers in front of him. "So what do we have here, detective?"

"A murder suspect, sir," Martin said. "I'd like to have him brought to Windsor for questioning."

Judge Senko nodded his head as he read the papers. "Alright, and why do you have two of these filled out?" he asked as he held up the second arrest warrant.

"Because we aren't sure if the suspect legally changed his name or if it's just a nickname," Martin replied.

The older man leaned back in his chair and looked thoughtfully at Martin for a moment. Then he closed his eyes for a few seconds. After he was done praying Judge Senko leaned back to his desk and signed the two papers. "Have these sent by courier to Toronto as soon as possible," Senko said. "And may God be with you."

Martin smiled and shook the judge's hand before he left the office.

"And may He give you wisdom in your decisions, sir."

Mike, Sara and Collette, walked into the Leddy Library at about noon. Sara and Mike attended their morning classes, and now they all had some free time, they decided to get their research done.

Mike went to get the article he found earlier and set it down in front of the girls. Sara scanned it quickly and then jotted down the names of the other two pastors involved in the debate.

One was Joseph Miller and the other was Kevin Moore, the pastor of the church that she and the others in the small group attended.

Mike said he would call Kevin, and Sara and Collette could find the phone number of the other Pentecostal pastor.

Collette quickly went to the section where the phone books were kept and grabbed one, within about two minutes they found the number for the pastor.

"I'll call," Sara said as she picked up a piece of paper and wrote the number down. Collette followed Sara down to the pay phones and to Mike.

Sara punched in the number and waited for someone to pick up the phone.

"Hello?" a female voice said.

"Hello," Sara replied. "I'm looking for Pastor Miller."

There was silence for a moment and then the female voice said softly, "I'm sorry, Pastor Miller died about three months ago, he had a heart attack."

Sara's face went blank. "I'm sorry to have bothered you madame."

Then she hung up.

"That only leaves Pastor Kevin," Mike said after Sara had related the new information.

Collette nodded. "And that means he's at risk."

"We should go see him," Sara said.

Mike put up his hands. "Now slow down here girls, we aren't the police. We should call Martin and find out what he wants us to do."

Collette sighed. "All right, Martin's coming over tonight after he's done work isn't he?"

Mike nodded.

"We can tell him then." Sara completed the thought.

Joanna led Jamie down the back steps and out into the yard, she pointed at a wooded pallet on the ground barely visible through the light cover of new falling snow ..

"There, that's the Pit," the small woman said softly. Jamie rushed over and removed the wooden lid.

"Marianne?" he said softly, once he heard the sobbing. "It's Jamie."

"Jamie?" Marianne said in reply. "How did you get here?"

"I came with Ben, David and Steve," Jamie replied, as he undid the coil of rope he brought from the car.

Silence. Then Marianne said, "They're dead."

Jamie paused, "How do you know that?" He lowered the rope into the Pit, handing some of the slack to Christine, whose face was ashen with fear. Jamie winked at her.

"Gerald told me at dinner tonight," Marianne said as she started to crawl up the sides of the hole.

Jamie reached down and pulled her up. Giving her a close, gentle hug he said, "Those guys are immortal, Gerald's lying," as he looked up at the rapidly burning house.

"Any more bright ideas, fearless leader?" Steve asked David as he stood at the top of the stairs staring down at the fierce flames that licked their way up to the second floor. David stared at the fire for a moment.

"David!" Ben yelled. "Standing and waiting for the fire is not an option!"

David shook his head and looked back at the hall. "We'll have to jump out a window," he said as he went back to one of the bedrooms.

"1 think I liked the standing idea better," Steve muttered.

David burst into a room and went to the window, ripped it open and looked outside. There he saw Jamie, Christine and Marianne running down the hill towards the Volvo. The horses were also wandering in the same general area, shying away from the flames.

"The girls! Jamie's got them!" David called back.

"So we came in here for nothing?" Ben said.

"You got to beat up Gerald," David replied as he leapt out the window. Each in turn jumped out and rolled along the snow to break the fall, They jumped onto the horses backs, Steve and Ben grunting as they did, and galloped towards the Volvo.

Jamie was searching the area for any signs of the three friends when the horses burst through the underbrush. Suddenly there they were, dirty, disheveled and tired, David, Ben and Steve were on the horses smiling down at Jamie and the girls. Jamie smiled, Marianne and Christine only stared.

"Gerald ... " Marianne started. "He said ... that you were all... dead."

David looked at Ben. "You're looking good for a dead guy."

"Must be the moisturizing cream," Ben laughed.

David got down off Yeshua and walked slowly to Marianne. "I thought that you were dead too," he said softly. "I didn't want to think what my life would be like without you." David cupped Marianne's face in his powerful, yet gentle hands. "I love you."

Marianne looked up and smiled. "I love you too. I didn't know it until 1 thought I'd lost you."

Jamie cleared his throat. "Uh, guys can we do this away from someone that wants to kill us?"

Marianne and David laughed and they all piled into the Volvo, the girls on each other's laps and Jamie, David and Ben in the front seat. Steve complained in the back about the leg room.

As Jamie rushed back to the airfield, Steve craned his head to look behind them.

"Guys?" he said urgently.

"What's up, Steve?" David asked.

Jamie glanced in the rear-view mirror. "Gerald," he said. Ben opened the window and stuck his head out. A bullet raced by him, narrowly missing his ear.

"Either that or a very peeved driver who doesn't like the way you drive," Ben said as he brought his head back in.

"We can do without the driving comments," Jamie said acidly. David turned in his seat, which left him almost on top of Ben.

"That car's easily going to catch us," he said.

Jamie swerved to keep Gerald's black car behind them. "Does anyone have any good news?"

"God's on our side," Marianne said.

"We got the girls back," David added.

Jamie shook his head in disgust, "That was a rhetorical question," he mumbled.

A shot was fired and the back glass was shattered, Steve grabbed the two girls and shoved them to the floor of the back seat.

"Sorry if it's uncomfortable," he muttered.

Ben reached out and angled the mirror on his side of the car so he could see Gerald's car.

"1 count three people in the car," he said.

Jamie glanced at his mirror. "Check," he said as he pulled the wheel hard to cut off the black sedan again

Another bullet whizzed by and cracked the windshield, causing a spider's web effect.

"That's starting to annoy me," David said.

Marianne reached up and grabbed David's hand, he looked down and smiled reassuringly at her and squeezed.

"We'll be fine," he whispered softly.

"Take the next left!" Ben yelled.

"Why?" Jamie asked.

"We don't want to bring a bunch of people into a populated city while their shooting guns," Ben said as he rummaged in the glove compartment.

"What are you hoping to find in there?" Steve asked.

"He's going to throw the book at them," Jamie said dryly. The others laughed weakly.

"There!" David said as he pointed to a small dirt road heading to the left.

A sudden rattle of bullets hit the back of the car and Ben whipped his head around to check everyone. He saw a small trickle of blood run down David's shoulder.

"That was an automatic weapon!" Jamie yelled.

"David's been hit!" Ben screamed.

"David!" Marianne yelled as she lifted her head.

"He's okay," Steve said as he pushed her back down. He leaned forward and started to clean the wound with a piece of cloth he ripped from his shirt.

David looked down at her, "I'm fine." He pulled his hand away from her and held it to his arm. "Hurts though."

Jamie suddenly smashed over the side of the road and into a field.

"Jamie?" Ben started. "What are you doing?"

"Cross country fleeing," Jamie said as he crashed the car over a rock. "If we're lucky they don't have snow tires."

Steve looked behind them and then suddenly dropped his head as another barrage of bullets hit the back of the car.

"It's not working!" he yelled.

Jamie angled the car back to the road. "Can't blame a guy for trying," he said.

As Jamie crashed the car back onto the road they sailed up on two wheels for a moment then, tipped onto their roof as the wheels skidded on the ice. A moment later they heard Gerald's car come to a halt behind them.

"Nice driving," Ben muttered. "There goes our deposit!"

"I didn't see you doing anything," Jamie replied.

Ben's door suddenly flew open and a strong arm pulled him out of the car. Ben looped his arm in his attacker's and jerked up. A loud crack told him it was broken, the gun in his hand dropped. Ben then smashed his fist into the man's jaw, he fell, unconscious.

David rolled out of the car grabbing and lifting the gun, pointing it back at Gerald and another man. The second man had his gun pointed at Ben.

"Drop your gun," Gerald said.

"Drop yours first, then I'll drop mine," David replied

Gerald laughed and walked forward. "You don't honestly think I believe you'll use that, do you?"

David shrugged his shoulders as he saw Ben walking up to his side. "I suppose you're right," David tossed the gun at the second man, he lowered his gun to catch it, and suddenly Ben was in motion, a well placed fist knocked the large man to the ground and a foot in the jaw knocked Gerald unconscious again. Ben stepped on the wrist of the black skinned man.

"Now, now, shooting people is not allowed," Ben said, just before he sent his fist into the man's jaw.

Jamie stumbled out of the car and looked around, dazed. "Thank you for riding Topsy-Turvy bus lines, please wait until the car has come to a complete stop before calling for help."

Steve and the girls were crawling out the back window and Steve glanced down at the three men on the ground.

"I assume they aren't going to get up for a while?" he asked.

"You assume right," Ben said, grimly.

Jamie walked over, ripping his shirt sleeve off, and looked at

David's shoulder. "Looks like it went right through the arm," he muttered as he pulled the makeshift bandage tight over Steve's.

"Yeah, I think so," David replied as he gave Marianne a hug with his good arm. "But I know I'll be fine now."

"Well," Steve said. "It was very nice of those people to leave us another car." He smiled at no one in particular, just a smile that said, can we please leave now?

After Jamie finished bandaging David's arm, they all got into Gerald's black car, it was much larger and more comfortable than the small Volvo. Ben found a cellular phone in the glove compartment and called the Police to pick up Gerald and the others. Then he called the rental agency to report the accident, and tell them where they could pick up the remains of the Volvo.

Jamie drove the small band back to the landing strip where The Skyhawk waited. Once there, they left the car, all piled into the plane, and sped into the air headed for home.

David and Marianne sat in the back of the plane, and talked softly with each other as they held hands. Christine fell asleep moments after they were in the air, and Steve was asleep shortly after her.

Ben and Jamie sat in the front of the plane, looking out on the white, frozen fields of the Northland.

"There!" Jamie exclaimed once they were in the air, "that wasn't so hard!"

Ben stared hard at his friend .

# Chapter Fifteen

That night after Bible study, Martin sat back in his chair with a broad smile on his face. "Guys, I sent off the arrest warrant for Robert Darkfall earlier today."

"That's great!" Mike said.

"We've got good news too," Sara said as she gave Martin a hug. "There's only one other pastor that was involved in the debate."

Martin smiled. "Good, that means it will be easier to keep him safe."

Just then the phone rang. Mike leaned over and answered it, smiling broadly when he heard the static-filled voice of Ben.

"Ben!" Mike said into the plastic receiver.

"This is costing money, Mike. We're still on the plane," Ben said. "I just wanted you guys to know we've got the girls and we're on our way home. And tell Sara I love her."

"Alright, Ben we'll see you in a bit," Mike said as he hung up the phone. "That was Ben, he was calling from the plane so he couldn't talk long, he just wanted to let us know they've got the girls and are on their way back." Then he turned to Sara, "And to tell you that he loved you."

Sara smiled and looked towards the kitchen. "I could use some tea. Anyone else?"

Pastor Kevin was a skinny man, and by no means a perfect physical specimen. He did, however have the kind of smile that was uncontrollably, and sometimes very annoyingly, contagious. On this night he was in his study, working on his sermon for the next Sunday.

As he worked, there was a knock on his door, and his wife, Marcia, entered. "There's a man in the foyer who wants to speak with you," she said. "Please be careful, I don't like the way he looks."

Kevin smiled at his wife and closed the reference book he was studying. As he walked out of the study he kissed his wife on the cheek. "You worry too much, dear."

As he walked up the hall, he held out his hand to the stranger dressed in black.

"Hello, I'm Pastor Kevin, can I help ... T" Kevin started then he paused as recognition flickered in his eyes.

"You remember me," Robert Darkfall said. "How pleasant."

Robert pulled a gun out from his coat and pointed it at Kevin. "We're going for a little ride."

Robert tied Kevin up and put him in the trunk of his car, then he returned and found Marcia trying to call the police.

"A little hard when I've cut the telephone lines, isn't it dear?" Robert said to the woman. Then he smashed her in the back of the head with the handle of his gun.

After he had tied Marcia up and left her in the bathtub, he slit her wrists, then raced to his rented car and squealed out of Kevin's driveway.

Mike reached over to grab the ringing phone. After he listened for a moment he handed the phone towards Martin.

"It's for you," Mike said.

Martin took the phone and soon his face went white. He slammed the receiver down onto the cradle and stormed to the closet, where his coat was.

"That was the office," he said as he put his coat on. "Robert Darkfall isn't at his house in Toronto. He did, however, have a ticket on the 2:00 pm train here."

"Pastor Kevin!" Mike said. "He's in danger!"

"The merely obvious will do, Mike," Martin said dryly. "The incredibly obvious is unnecessary."

"Let me call his home first," Sara said. "He might be at the church."

Martin nodded and Mike reached for his coat and threw it on.

"Where do you think you're going?" Martin said.

"With you," Mike replied.

"No, you're not," Martin commanded. "I'll not risk any lives on this case. It's one thing to help with the legwork but this could be dangerous."

"It's not your decision, Martin," Mike retorted. "It's mine."

Martin studied Mike's, stern face for a moment and then threw his hands in the air. "1 give up!" he said.

Sara put the phone down. "There's no answer at the house," she reported. "They must be at the church."

Martin thought for a moment. "Well, all the other murders have happened at churches. Even if he did go to the house first, he'd probably have brought the pastor to the church to kill him, on a cross, like the others."

Mike opened the door and looked back at Martin. "Let's go we're wasting time."

Martin looked back at the girls. "I'll call a few cars to his house, just in case. You girls stay here. If we're not back in three hours, call the police to the church."

Sara nodded and gave Martin a quick hug. "God bless," she whispered softly into his ear.

"We'll need it," Martin replied with a smile.

Martin raced down the street, siren blaring until he turned up the side street leading to the church. Then he flipped the siren and the headlights off.

"I'll go in the front," Martin told Mike. "You come in after me. If Darkfall runs, you go help the pastor, I'll get Darkfall."

Mike nodded, his hands were clammy and he was starting to wonder if it had been a good idea for him to come along in the first place.

Martin wheeled into the parking lot of the church and stopped at the front entrance. He jumped out and quickly pulled his service revolver out of its holster, holding it ready in front of his face.

Mike followed Martin up the steps to the front doors and waited as Martin slowly opened them and slipped in. Mike followed him closely.

Mike's thoughts were suddenly invaded by life, and death and he wondered if he was truly ready to face either. He heard the stories David and Ben told about the churches and what the murders looked like. His greatest fear right now was walking into the sanctuary of the church and finding Pastor Kevin looking like the other pastor, that Ben and David described.

As they entered the sanctuary, they heard Pastor Kevin pleading with Robert not to hurt him any more. Then they heard the sound of a metal on metal and Kevin screamed.

Martin kicked the sanctuary doors opened and screamed, "Freeze, this is the police!"

Robert turned, a bloody hammer in his hand. He threw the hammer at Martin, and raced out a side door. Martin ran after Robert at full speed.

"See to the Pastor!" Martin yelled back, as he bolted through the door.

Mike ran up the aisle and crouched beside Kevin.

"Stay still," Mike told the bleeding pastor. "I'll get help." Mike ripped his shirt off and packed it around the one nail Robert managed to pound through Kevin's wrist.

Mike ran back to the church office and ripped it open. He picked up the phone, quickly dialed 911, and asked for an ambulance and police.

Then he returned to Kevin and found him lying quietly on the cross which used to hang on the wall behind the pulpit.

"How did you know?" Kevin asked.

"We didn't really," Mike explained. "It was just a hunch that he was coming here to kill you, you were the last one on the list of the clergy who participated in the debate. It was really just God's hand in our lives

"Well, I for one am glad for that," Kevin said weakly from the floor.

Martin raced out the side door from the sanctuary, his gun out and ready, pointing it in all directions around him, scanning the area with his well trained eyes. The room was dark and it took a moment for his eyes to adjust to the lack of light. As he heard a door close behind him, he spun around and leaped to the door, kicking it with his foot he pointed his gun in and scanned the area again.

Robert was standing just off to the side, he crashed his hand down onto Martin's gun, sending it flying up the hall. Martin quickly reacted with a punch that Robert easily blocked, and a kick that missed its mark.

Robert brought his knee up and hit Martin in the side, he doubled over. Martin brought his fist up again and caught Robert in the cheek under his left eye. Robert fumbled back, ducked down to grab something and turned at a run.

Martin spent a few seconds scanning for his gun, but couldn't find it in the dark room, before he ran off to follow Robert.

After following him through the church Martin crashed out one of the back doors and saw Robert running up the street towards a dark car.

"Stop! Police!" Martin called.

"Or you'll shoot?" Robert called back as he waved something small in the air.

Martin took a few more steps towards Robert before he watched him speed away in the night.

Ben climbed off the plane in Toronto, followed by David, Marianne, Christine, Steve and Jamie. It was dark in Toronto and the small group hadn't slept much in the two days they were away. They walked in a strange daze that left them both weary and at the same time unwilling to release themselves to the uncertainties of sleep. Steve and Christine woke up shortly after they had fallen asleep, complaining about nightmares. David and Marianne prayed with them but the two young people couldn't fall asleep for the rest of the trip to Toronto.

"I'll go see to the plane's refueling," Jamie said as he trudged off in the direction of the fuel tankers.

Steve looked around and then went off in the direction of his office. "I'm going to make sure the fuel is covered by the company."

Marianne and David sat together on a bench and whispered softly to each other about their experiences in Timmins. Christine had shared with the others on the plane about the woman named Joanna, and how she left the Bible in the room for Christine. Also how Joanna and she were able to visit a few more times and they were able to read the Bible together, and share with a great deal about the Lord, and about her family. Now she laid curled up on a chair and tried to get some rest.

Ben walked over to the window and watched as Jamie oversaw the refueling process. He started this trip with David in the sanctuary of Assumption church. Ben watched David as he went through his own personal spiritual problems. David didn't know Ben could tell he was having problems, but he knew. And Ben had been praying for David the entire time. Ben watched David as he struggled with the rights and wrongs of how the cult subculture dealt with things. Ben prayed for David too. He watched as David dealt with the possibility that Marianne, the woman he loved might be killed. And Ben was there to pray for David. Now, he looked over to David and Marianne as they held each others hands and he smiled at their happiness. But why do I feel so bad about this? Ben asked himself that question over and over again.

It wasn't over yet, and Ben feared that the worse was yet to come. He watched as Jamie headed back to the hanger and waved at Ben. Ben waved back weakly and smiled even weaker.

"Alright guys, let's get you home," Jamie said as he walked into the waiting room. Steve followed a step behind the young blond man.

"I want to call them first," Ben said. He walked over to a phone and dialed home. After the third ring Sara answered.

"Hi, Blossom," Ben said. "Yes, I'm fine, I just wanted to call and tell you we'll be home about midnight." Then Ben said good bye and sighed.

David dashed over to a small variety store. Ben noticed that whatever he bought he tucked into his coat.

"What's that?" Ben said as they followed Jamie, Steve and the girls out to the tarmac.

David lifted his coat and showed Ben the single, red rose, wrapped in plastic and tucked into his coat by his heart. "I'm going to give it to Marianne tonight when we say good night," he said with a smile. "I wanted a white one but they only had red."

Ben smiled and clapped David on the back. "I'm sure that'll be fine."

Steve, David, Marianne and Christine climbed into the plane and then Jamie and Ben took their seats.

"Okay," Jamie said. "Let's go."

"Home," David said softly. "It seems so far away."

"Nonsense," Jamie replied. "It's just a hop, skip and a jump from here."

When Mike and Martin returned to the house Sara was just about ready to call the police.

"We saved Pastor Kevin, but Robert got away," Mike reported to the girls.

"Well, I've got some more good news," Sara said. "Ben and the others should be back in about half an hour."

Martin sat in his usual chair by the fireplace and smiled. "Okay, we'll go pick them up in a few then."

"What happens with Robert?" Collette asked.

Martin stretched. "Well, there's an APB out on him right now. He can't leave the country or go anywhere where he'll have to show ID. We'll have him soon."

Mike stood and walked over to the window, staring out at the swirling snow.

Sara walked up behind him, and tapped his shoulder.

"You okay?" she asked.

"Just thinking about Christine," Mike said softly. "Just thinking about what's going to happen when she gets back. I don't know."

"I don't think you're supposed to know, Mike," Collette said as she went to get the coats for everyone.

"I think this should have been a learning experience for everyone involved," Martin said. "What did you learn, Mike?"

Mike turned and looked at Martin hard for a moment. "I learned that a few miles is nothing compared to a lifetime of love." Then he smiled sadly. "If only I could believe it now."

Martin stood and stretched his large body. "We should go get them now," he said as he walked towards the door.

Robert sat in his rented car and watched as Martin stepped outside and slid into his Oldsmobile. A few seconds later Sara and Mike came out as well, and followed him.

Robert watched as Martin pulled the car out and drove it down the street. He lifted the gun that he picked up off the floor at the church and turned it in his hand, admiring the smooth, heavy feel of it. Then he turned his car on and pulled out after Martin.

A few seconds later, Charles pulled his car out into traffic behind

Robert. Raven sat in the passenger seat and watched with interest as the small caravan made its way to the airport.

"It ends tonight, Charles," Raven said to his companion. Charles wordlessly followed Robert's car.

"A few years ago, I would have been in that car with Robert," Raven continued. "We were friends once. Then something happened. I have no idea what, but there became something cruel and wicked inside him. While it was still an investigation of the unknown for me."

Raven looked out the window and a picture appeared in his head, a picture of three friends, canoing down a long clear stream. "Time changes many things, Charles," Raven said. "It changes mountains, and landscapes, and people. I think it changes people the most. They become exactly what they never wanted to be."

"That's a very sad view of things, Raven," Charles replied. "I like to think time can change people for the better too."

Raven thought for a moment, then smiled. "Perhaps," he said, thinking about the long haired young man, once called Gideon. "Perhaps it can change people for the better as well."

Martin pulled his car into the airport parking lot and followed the others into the foyer.

Waiting for them was the ragtag group from their not so wonderful adventure, after Marianne and Christine. Sara ran and held Ben close to her.

"I love you," she said into his ear.

"I know, Blossom," Ben replied softly. "I know."

Mike stood beside Martin, a great relief was lifted from him when he saw Christine. He slowly moved forward and when he reached out to touch her he immediately pulled her close to him in an embrace.

"I'm so happy your safe," he said, tears flowing down his face in rivers.

"I'm just glad you're holding me again," Christine replied.

"You guys look tired," Martin said. "Let's get you home." Martin turned out of the airport and into the cold wind.

Robert slammed his car door shut and lifted Martin's gun up, pointing it through the swirling snow, and into the little group leaving the airport.

"Die, scum!" Robert screamed as he pulled the trigger. The gun fired, and Martin was blown back and into Mike and Christine. Ben jumped forward and felt for Martin's gun, but couldn't find it.

Robert ran towards Ben and laid the nozzle of the gun on Ben's temple. Ben stood and faced Robert for the first time. His eyes widened as he saw Kriston's face.

"Kristen?" Ben asked, surprised.

"Not any more," Robert said, his voice taking on a totally different tone, one of evil and hatred. "1 am Robert Darkfall, and I am about to kill you."

Using what strength he had left in his weak body, Ben swung his head back, and rolled out onto the snow. Robert followed with his gun and pulled the trigger.

Ben heard the gunshot, but felt nothing but a weight on his body.

He looked down and saw David's face, staring blankly at him.

Pushing the sudden sickening bile that filled his throat down Ben rolled again, and popped up to his feet. Robert was running at him, pointing the gun still. Ben fell and rolled into Robert's legs. The gun skittered on the ice towards the parking lot. Robert fell over Ben's body and forced himself to his feet while reaching into his pocket for the knife he used to kill Joshua.

Ben's head swam in fatigue and pain. The wound Gerald gave him in Timmins was open again and he could feel the blood running down his arm. Somewhere around him, he heard Marianne screaming for an ambulance and Martin saying he was fine and had to get to David. As his eyes started to clear, he saw Mike moving towards him with an agility that defied his large frame. Steve ran into the airport again, and the girls, Martin and Jamie were crowded around David's inert form.

Robert suddenly appeared swinging his hand down at Ben's head.

Suddenly it stopped and Mike's massive hand held it steady in the air, Ben noticed the wicked looking knife it held. Robert swung his other hand across and cracked it into Mike's jaw sending him falling into the snow on the parking lot.

Ben brought one of his legs around and into Robert's knee bringing him to the snow once again. As he stumbled to his feet, Ben could feel Robert getting up and turned on one knee to face another attack.

He turned just in time to block a punch with his forearm. Robert brought his knife hand down, and Ben leaned back, then suddenly reeled as pain ran down his face.

Robert stood and followed his prey as Ben rolled and crawled his

way out into the open parking lot, where he hoped his martial arts training would be of more use.

"I've won, Gideon," Robert was saying. "Face it. You're about to die."

Ben stood and faced Robert, blood streaming down his face where Robert's blade had cut a long ragged slash through his left eye. Ben's right eye squinted through blood and pain, and he saw Robert closing in like a wolf for a kill.

Suddenly, another gunshot rang out and Robert fell onto his back.

Ben looked behind him and saw Raven walking towards him carrying Martin's gun.

"People should not leave these things lying about," he said, yet there was no humor in his face.

Ben turned again, wordlessly, and stumbled to David's body.

"David," Marianne was saying as she cradled his head in her lap. "I love you."

David's face was pale, his blood soaked the snow. His eyes were heavy as he looked up to her.

"I love you too, Sweetheart," he said softly. He reached into his coat and pulled out the rose, which was battered and covered in blood.

"I wanted to give you this. I'm sorry, I was looking for a white one, but..." He suddenly coughed and blood trickled from his lips. He pushed the bloody rose into Marianne's hands.

Marianne looked up and buried her face into Sara's shoulder, her body racking with sobs. "This was it," she sobbed into Sara's ear. "This rose was the sign."

Ben looked over to Martin, whose arm was soaked in his own blood. Martin glanced at him and ripped out the lining of his coat, pressing it against Ben's face.

"He was shot in the spine. I think it hit his lung too," Martin said softly, he pulled Ben close and whispered in his ear, "He's drowning in his own blood." Then he turned to David. "Ben's here, David, he's okay."

David looked up at Ben and smiled weakly. "Good thing too," he said. Then he looked down to his feet. "My legs are so cold." Then he laid his head back on Marianne's lap.

Ben stood up and pulled the bandage off his face, handing it to Sara. "I'll be back," he said to her.

As he walked towards Robert's body, he heard David's voice, a raspy gurgle, "I'm so tired."

Raven was kneeling beside Robert's body talking softly with him as Ben shuffled up.

Ben knelt beside Robert and propped his head up.

"Kriston?" Ben said softly. "Kriston, can you hear me?"

"It's too late, Gideon. He's too far gone," Raven said, as he glanced up to Ben's face, there were tears in his eyes. "Are you okay?"

"I'll be fine," Ben replied.

Robert moved on the ground and his eyes opened. Ben looked down and saw they were soft and clear, like they used to be. He forced a smile as he looked down at his friend.

"Raven. Gideon. Where am I?" Kriston said.

"Kriston?" Raven said disbelief dripping from his voice.

"1...1... want to go away, Raven," Kriston said. "1 want... to sleep."

"Be at peace, my friend," Raven said softly into Kriston's ear.

"Lightbringer. .. " Kriston said softly, blood running out his mouth. "What happened to ... ?"

"The Lightbringer is gone, Kris," Ben interrupted. He felt something wet on his lips and licked them. It was salty, then he realized he was crying.

"1... was wrong, Gideon," Kriston continued. "To join ... the cult. I should have been like you. I should have followed ... your Jesus."

"You still can, Kris," Ben said. "You still can .. "

# Chapter Sixteen

Ben stood in the cold wind with Raven and a few of Kriston's family as they watched the funeral director slowly lower the coffin into the ground. Raven turned and started walking towards his car with Ben following close behind.

"Need a ride?" Raven asked.

"We're not far from my house," Ben replied. "I think I'll just walk."

Raven turned to face Ben. "What happened, Gideon? It used to be so much fun, so ... exciting."

Ben shook his head. "Satan always makes it seem fun and exciting before he gets his claws into you."

Raven nodded and got into his car. "I'll see you around, Gideon."

"I know you will," Ben said softly as he watched the dark car pull away.

David Masterson's funeral was quiet and peaceful, just as David had been. He was buried in his home town of Elmira, just north-west of Toronto, a picturesque country village. He laid in a black lacquered casket, with brass handles. Ben looked up into the overcast sky and thought he could imagine David in Heaven, walking hand in hand with Jesus down the golden street. Then suddenly Jesus talked within Ben's image in his head. Ben saw Him turn to David and draw him into a warm hug and say, "Greater love has no one than this, that he lay down his life for his friends" (John 15:13).

Ben suddenly broke into tears and turned away.

Jamie left for Toronto the day before the funeral, saying he wished he could stay but had work to do, places to fly. Ben secretly thought Jamie just couldn't bear to cry in front of other people. That was the kind of thing Jamie wished to do alone.

Steve stayed with the group for a few days after the funeral. He said it was to help them, but they all knew that it was for his health as well.

Collette took a train from Elmira to Toronto, after the funeral. She told them they would always be in her prayers and she hoped to see them again soon.

Christine came back with the group, saying she would like to visit for a week or so. Ben thought she just wanted to fall in love with Mike again; that thought made him smile.

"Ben," said Martin that evening as they visited Pastor Kevin, who was recuperating at home. "What were you, Raven and Robert, or Kriston, or whoever doing while we were still at the airport?"

Ben sighed and took a long drink of the Earl Grey tea Marcia served him. "1 was helping him accept the Lord, Martin. After he asked whether the Lightbringer was gone he wanted to rest, he said he was wrong and should have followed me. I told him it wasn't me he should follow, but God instead."

Ben sat a little while longer, then added, "He wasn't really a bad person, Kriston I mean. Robert Darkfall was a totally different person, to me."

"What was Kriston like?" Sara asked.

Ben thought for a moment. "He was much like David was." Then he looked at Marianne'S shocked expression. "Before he became Robert Darkfall, he was much like David. Gentle and caring, and very much at peace with himself."

Pastor Kevin put his good hand around Marcia, whose wrists were bandaged. She had come to in the bathtub and managed to stop the bleeding from the careless attempt on her life. Kevin kissed Marcia on the cheek, then looked at Martin. "What happened to this Raven guy?"

Martin smiled. "He was let go because he used the gun to save a life."

Ben scratched at the bandage on his face until Sara slapped his hand. "Yeah," he said with an annoyed look at Sara. "He has quit his position with the cult of Ctchutic."

"Praise God!" Pastor Kevin exclaimed.

"Not yet," Ben continued. "He hasn't yet accepted Jesus as Saviour."

"It's a start, Ben," Pastor Kevin said. "We should praise God for every little blessing we receive."

They sat in silence for a little while. Then Mike tapped Ben on the shoulder.

"Ben," he said. "You said Kriston asked if the Lightbringer was gone. Who were you talking about?"

Ben thought for a moment, trying to remember the story. "Before Lucifer Morningstar was banished from Heaven, he was the most lovely of all the Angels. He was Lucifer Morningstar, the Lightbringer. He was powerful and proud and the greatest of all the angels. That's just a story they tell to make Satan seem more powerful than he really is. They also say he was more powerful than the Son of God, and that Jesus was jealous of him. They don't understand that God is the three in one.

"I think Kriston got too into getting the power that comes with the Occult and was taken over completely by one of Satan's minions."

"If the daemon was one of Satan's stooges than why did it call itself The Lightbringer?" Martin asked.

"Daemon's will do that, Martin," Pastor Kevin said. "They also want to appear more powerful than they really are."

"That's sad," Marianne said softly. "That anyone would call out to Satan, for power, and not call out to God, a being of pure love and forgiveness. He created everything anyway, so He's really all-powerful."

"Yes, it is," Ben agreed. "But it happens, every day."

"Ben said something about God being three in one," Martin said to

Pastor Kevin. "I still don't get that." Martin had accepted Jesus into his heart the day before David's funeral, and everyone was excited about helping him understand everything. They enjoyed watching his growth and that re-enforced and reminded them, and increased their own knowledge.

"Well," Pastor Kevin started. "It's like water. It can be ice, liquid or steam. Three different things, but always the same."

"And He's always there for us," Steve said. "He'll never leave, like the Lightbringer."

THE END

# THE NEXT INSTALLMENT OF THE STORY

*Coming some time in 2020!*

This ends the first book of what I have started calling the "U-Crew" series. I say first because I already have plans for another story, where I'll delve into a different and engaging problem that Christian youth are dealing with today. What is this? I'm not telling, right now but I'm hoping to have it complete and for sale by early to mid 2020. God willing. I enjoyed going on this little trip wigth these characters and I am looking forward to working with them again in a new book. But I do have a few other irons in the fire right now. The Forgotten is a story about a Christian run group home and the problems those workers face every day. That sould be out in 2019 at some point. The Desk is still in it's infancy, but it will follow in the same style as The Janitor did. Lots of flashbacks and a character driven plot. I look forward to sharing these with you.

God bless you and keep you,
Douglas Scaddan
December 13th, 2018

# About The Author

Douglas Scaddan lives in Kitchener, Ontario, Canada. He is a Developmental Service Worker for Christian Horizons, a non profit organization that is dedicated to serving people with exceptional needs.

He loves his job.

He enjoys writing about things that have meaning and maybe a little bit of controversy in them. His Soldiers of God series explores the needs of soldiers that return from service with problems they never even knew they had.

He enjoys reading, writing and working out. The latter he sometimes finds difficult to gather motivation for.

# Coming Soon!

***From Douglas Scaddan Publishing***
***It takes a man of God to love***

## *The Forgotten*

# Coming Summer 2019!

www.ingramcontent.com/pod-product-compliance
Lightning Source LLC
LaVergne TN
LVHW050534100826
845148LV00002B/553

* 9 7 8 0 9 6 8 3 0 7 1 4 4 *